D1483603

Gospel, Catechesis, Catechism

JOSEPH CARDINAL RATZINGER

Gospel, Catechesis, Catechism

Sidelights on the
Catechism of the Catholic Church

IGNATIUS PRESS   SAN FRANCISCO

Title of the German original:
Evangelium—Katechese—Katechismus
Streiflichter auf den Katechismus der katholischen Kirche
© 1995 Verlag Neue Stadt GmbH, Munich

Cover design by Roxanne Mei Lum

Contents

Preface

Two years after the publication of the *Catechism of the Catholic Church*, a significant portion of German-language theology still tends to "shut out" the book and to declare it a fundamental mistake. Meanwhile, there is no overlooking the fact that the Christian world has pronounced a very different judgment. Wherever it is published, the *Catechism* generates a demand that puzzles not only sociologists and pollsters but even Church officials and catechetical experts. Although explanations of the phenomenon may differ on points of detail, one thing is certain: the *sensus fidei* of the People of God is coming to expression here in a way that can no longer be ignored. If, on the other hand, the group of theologians just mentioned does not want to find itself increasingly "shut out" of this worldwide development of the *sensus fidei*, it will eventually have to relax its negative posture. It will have to engage the *Catechism* positively, and that means bringing to it more than the lenses of the schoolmaster. The four chapters of this small volume are meant as an invitation to this changed approach to the *Catechism*. The pieces that appear here are far from being in any way complete; they are occasional writings, sidelights on individual aspects of the *Catechism*. But perhaps for this very reason they will be able to encourage an unprejudiced reading of the work as a whole. These modest essays will have attained their purpose if they inspire a willingness to read the *Catechism* with this open-minded attitude.

+ Joseph Cardinal Ratzinger
Rome, July 31, 1994

What Can We Expect from a Catechism of the Catholic Church?

The *Catechism of the Catholic Church*[1] is the end result of an approximately six-year-long collaborative effort that brought together bishops, theologians and laymen. In the Apostolic Constitution that introduces the *Catechism*, the Pope rightly speaks of the text's many-voiced harmony, noting that it truly "expresses what could be called the 'symphony' of the faith". The Pope adds that "the achievement of this *Catechism* thus reflects

[1] "World Catechism" [*Weltkatechismus*] has largely become the dominant term in German-speaking countries. This may work as a shorthand expression, but it implies a somewhat dubious shift with respect to the original title. The *Catechism* is a book of and for the entire Church; only through the living Church does it also speak to the world. Numerous controversies cease to be important when this distinction is kept clearly in view. For example, the remarks that B. J. Hilberath has felt obliged to offer concerning the *Catechism*'s genesis and purpose (B. J. Hilberath, "Ein Katechismus für die ganze Welt?") in *ThQ* 173 (1993): 312f., completely miss the real truth. Hilberath speaks of a Roman Catechism "that aids and abets the confusion between faith and its expression" and thus brashly tosses off the verdict that "the local churches no more need this kind of catechism than the African Synod needs the Vatican as a meeting place!" (313). This sounds very grand to a German readership. The only difficulty is that all of the numerous African bishops with whom I had the chance to speak told me that, as a matter of fact, their Synod did need Peter's See as a meeting place. A little later, Hilberath says: "But the claim of Vatican officials to be able to superintend the whole

the collegial nature of the Episcopate; it testifies to the Church's catholicity."

The response to the *Catechism* reflects and confirms its origin. Wherever it has appeared on the shelves, the *Catechism* has become a smashing success. In France, it became an overnight best-seller that one could purchase in airport bookstalls and railway stations among items that one would not normally associate with a catechism. In the Spanish- and Portuguese-speaking world, even people who generally do not read were clamoring for it. It was not long before a whole body of extracts and summaries began springing up.

Despite a far-reaching propaganda campaign against the *Catechism*, it generated a great demand in the German-speaking countries. Perhaps the most spectacular success of all was reserved for the English edition. The subtlety of the English language, its worldwide diffusion in various cultural contexts, developments in feeling for language [*sprachgefühl*], and the evolution of

---

operation from central headquarters is presumptuous, not to mention fraught with dangerous consequences" (317). I, for one, do not know the "Vatican officials" who make this claim. In any case, the *Catechism* was not written in this way but precisely in the way that Hilberath describes as the ideal earlier on in the article. The gathering flood of faith testimonies from the local churches was sifted by their representatives and fitted together into a whole. The end result was a "truly catholic catechism". It is a shame that Hilberath did not take the time to find out how the *Catechism* really was produced.

speech-related ideologies had slowed down the process of translation. As a result, the English-language version of the *Catechism* could not be published until the early summer of 1994—first in Africa, then in Great Britain, Ireland and the United States of America. Further editions (of the same text) will appear in India, the Philippines and in other English-speaking countries. In England, 100,000 copies of the *Catechism* were sold within two weeks of its publication, and the demand remains steady. In the United States, half a million copies had already been ordered even before the book was available on the market. To date more than two million copies have been sold. Further translations, especially into the Slavic languages, are underway.

Chief among the versions still in preparation is the Latin, which will become the *textus typicus*, the standard text against which all the translations will have to be checked. It may seem odd that the standard text will appear last. However, this affords the commission in charge of the *Catechism* another opportunity to go through all the citations and cross-references. It will also give the commission a chance to study and take into account all comments on oversights, occasional imprecise formulations, and the like, that do not call into question the substance of the text itself. The Latin text will not be a modified version, a sort of new revised edition. With the approbation bestowed by the papal constitution of October 11, 1992, the French version was recognized as the definitive form of the text.

What are possible and expected, however, are stylistic improvements (where the context does not appear completely clear) and corrections (where there are mistakes in citations or other sorts of inaccuracies in the historical documentation).

Various extracts from the *Catechism* were already circulating even before the publication of the official text in December 1992. The selection of these extracts was generally rather tendentious, and the texts themselves were almost universally based on provisional versions. This had the disadvantage of spreading inexact, indeed, distorted ideas about the book. Yet it also had a positive side, insofar as it stimulated curiosity about the real contents of the work. Almost without exception, these prepublications pounced on the moral part of the *Catechism*. Readers could easily have gotten the impression that the *Catechism* was nothing but a catalogue of sins. The unauthorized publications often made it appear as though the Church mainly wanted to tell people what they could not do and that she had a fixation on sin. Nevertheless, this very fact sparked a lively debate. For while it is certainly neither possible nor desirable to live by prohibitions and accusations, the question about our duty as human beings, about the kind of life required for the rectitude of our own being and the being of the world, is the essential question of every age. And precisely the men of our time, who face so many catastrophes and menaces, yet are also in search of real hope, experience it with renewed passion as the fundamental question that concerns each and every one of us.

J. P. Sartre regarded it as man's basic drama, indeed, tragedy, that he is thrown into a freedom that leaves him to determine what he ought to do with his existence. But this is precisely what man is ignorant of, and every time he makes a decision he plunges into an adventure of uncertain outcome. It seems to me that so many contemporary thinkers and artists dedicated themselves to Marxism because, whatever its flaws, it gave a coherent and, on its own premises, logical answer to this basic human problem, while seeming to put all the energies of our existence at the service of a great moral purpose: the creation of a better humanity and a better world. In reality, however, this Marxism was for many only a palliative to dull the feeling of meaninglessness and aimlessness that afflicted them.

The collapse of ideologies has put fresh discussion of the question of man and morality back on the agenda. What ought we to do? How does our life find its proper course? What gives us and the world as a whole a future worth living? Because the *Catechism* deals with these questions, it reaches beyond the merely intramural concerns of theology or the Church to touch everyone. One significant reason why it can expect to meet with interest is that, instead of representing a private opinion concocted by this or that individual, it

draws its answer to these questions from a vast trea-
sury of communal experience. But this experience in
turn rests upon observations transcending the merely
human, observations that transmit what was seen and
heard by men who were in contact with God himself.

After what I have said so far, someone might ask
whether the *Catechism* is a moral treatise after all. The
answer is this: The *Catechism* is about morality, but
about much more, too. It deals with man, but its treatment reflects the conviction that it is impossible to sep-
arate the question of man from the question of God.
We do not speak rightly about man unless we also speak
about God. But we cannot speak rightly about God unless God himself tells us who he is. For this reason, the
moral instruction offered by the *Catechism* cannot be
severed from what the text says concerning God and
God's history with us. The *Catechism* must be read as a
unity. We misread the passages concerned with morality when we detach them from their context, that is,
from the Creed and from the doctrine of the sacraments. For the *Catechism*'s fundamental anthropologi-
cal proposition is that man is created in God's image
and is thus like God. Everything the text says about
the rectitude of human behavior rests upon the recognition of this central truth. This truth also grounds
those rights that are inherent in man from conception
to the final moment of his existence. No one has to
give man these rights, no one can take them from him:

he has them of himself. It follows that the image of God is also the basis of human dignity, which in every man is inviolable simply because he is man. Finally, man's Godlikeness also implies the unity and equality of men. As creatures of the one God, all men are of the same rank, are related to one another as brothers, are responsible for one another and are called to love their neighbor, no matter who he may be.

As the *Catechism* sees things, then, the question of man and the question of God are inextricably woven together. The text is able to make all its affirmations about our moral conduct only in the perspective of God, the God who has revealed himself in Jesus Christ.

However, it also becomes clear that this conception of morality is not an accumulation of prohibitions or a catalogue of sins. The question at stake is always: How do I achieve rectitude as a human being, how do I make my life turn out for the best [*gelingen*]? On this point, the *Catechism* clearly favors the Augustinian conception of morality, whose basic approach is very simple. As he pursued the tangled paths of his life, Augustine constantly asked himself one question: How do I attain happiness? This is a question we all ask; the longing for happiness is ingrained in our very being.

Drawing on the faith of the Church, the *Catechism* tells us that happiness can be had only together with others and in responsibility for the whole of humanity. In the end, however, men can be in communion with, and take responsibility for, one another only when man is in communion with God and responsible to him. In this sense, morality is a doctrine about the nature of happiness and the means to attain it—not an egoistic, pseudohappiness, to be sure, but the genuine reality.

Moreover, the *Catechism*'s essential answer to these questions is also very simple. In unison with the Bible and the faith of the Church, the *Catechism* affirms that man's happiness is love. In this sense, the morality of the *Catechism* is a teaching about the nature of love. What the *Catechism* tells us on this point is that the essence of true love has been manifested visibly in the Person of Jesus Christ: in his words, but also in his life and death. It also tells us that the Ten Commandments merely unfold the ways of love and that we understand the Decalogue correctly only when we read it together with Jesus Christ. All the essential points of the Creed thus converge and become praxis in the moral part of the *Catechism*. For its moral doctrine takes as its starting point the yearning for happiness and love that the Creator has placed in each of our hearts.

These considerations also bring to light the significance of the *imago Dei*. Man is like God in that he is capable of love and truth. Moral conduct is therefore in the deepest sense of the word conduct in harmony with creation. When the Catholic moral tradition and, in its wake, the *Catechism* speak of the nature of man, of the natural law and of behavior in conformity with nature, what is meant is not some form of biologism but behavior that accords with what the Creator has implanted in the core of our being. If we continue this line of inquiry, we discover love as the heart of all morality; and if we then delve more deeply into this love, we meet Christ, the incarnate love of God.

I have dwelt on the *Catechism*'s moral vision as long as I have, not in order to isolate morality again, but, on the contrary, to awaken interest in the work as a whole, even where it does not answer immediately to present-day curiosity. In this spirit, I would like to add a couple of brief observations regarding the other parts of the *Catechism* as well as to point out a few particularities in its structure.

Like baptismal catechesis from the earliest times, the first part is patterned on the Creed. In particular, it takes as its model the so-called "Apostles' Creed", which began in the early centuries as the Roman Church's baptismal creed and then spread out from Rome to become a standard for the whole of Western Christianity. However, its essential structure and its various articles accord entirely with Eastern baptismal creeds. Therefore, our adoption of the Apostles' Creed as a pattern for the *Catechism* cannot be judged as a one-sided privileging of Western tradition. A tradition dating back to the fourth century divides the Apostles' Creed into twelve articles corresponding to the number of the apostles. There is definitely a point to this division, but the original structure of this creed is simpler. As a baptismal creed, the *Apostolicum*, like the baptismal formula, is an altogether simple profession of faith in the three-in-one God: the Father, the Son and the Holy Spirit. We decided to retain this ternary structure common to all baptismal creeds. This option brings out very nicely the hierarchy of truths: in the end, Christian faith is simply faith in God. Everything else is an unfolding of that. Our faith is not a theory but an event, an encounter with the living God who is our Father, who in his Son Jesus Christ has assumed human nature, who unites us in the Holy Spirit and who, in all this, remains the one and only God. The linking of the doctrine of the faith to the baptismal profession of faith also makes it clear that catechesis is not simply the communication of a religious theory. Rather, it intends to set a life-process in motion: namely, growth in the life given through baptism, growth in communion with God.

In this way, the first part passes over naturally into the second, which presents the seven sacraments. The sacraments are the Church in action. All the religions of history have had sacred signs. Man can touch the eternal only in sensible realities, but the things of this world are also intrinsically designed to mediate contact with God. Faith could therefore take over the signs of creation and the symbolic cosmos prepared by the religions, just as these signs and symbols could, in obedience to Christ's command, become signs of the redemption. For this reason, we always tried to present the sacraments in terms of their liturgical form. This second part of the *Catechism* is thus simultaneously an initiation into the liturgy of the Church.

Our difficulty was that, in a book intended for the whole Church, we could not simply assume one given rite, for example, the Latin rite, as our starting point. Concrete application to individual rites must occur in catechesis. We endeavored to set forth the basic framework common to the various rites. This was not always easy, but it proved to be a fascinating enterprise: one can see how, amid the great variety of liturgical forms, the dominant symbols are nonetheless common and thus manifest the will of Christ himself.

In a certain sense, the fourth part, which is devoted to prayer, recapitulates the preceding parts: prayer is applied faith. It is inseparably tied to the world of the sacraments. On the one hand, the sacraments presuppose personal prayer. On the other hand, they guarantee it a stable orientation, inserting it into the common prayer of the Church and thus into Christ's dialogue with the Father. But prayer and morality are also inseparable: only when man turns to God does he find the paths leading to his true being. From prayer we continually receive the correction we need; reconciliation with God makes possible reconciliation among ourselves.

However, the *Catechism* gives its teaching on prayer,

whose core is a commentary on the Our Father in the line of the great catechetical traditions, a further significance: prayer is the expression of our hope. The fact that we must pray, that we must make petitions, shows that our life and our world are imperfect and in need of superior help. The fact that we may and can pray shows that we have the gift of hope, the hope we find summed up in the words "thy kingdom come." When we make this request, we are praying for the present world, but we are praying at the same time for eternal life, for the new world. We thus see in the four parts of the *Catechism* the interplay of faith, hope and love. Because we believe, we dare to hope; because we believe and hope, we can love.

In conclusion, let me add a few technical directions for reading the *Catechism*.

Historical information and supplementary doctrinal explanations are found in small print. They can be skipped over by readers with less specialized interest.

However, a fairly large number of short, easily remembered texts from the Fathers, the liturgy, the Magisterium and the history of the Church also appear in small print. These texts are meant to convey some sense of the wealth and beauty of the faith. We took care to maintain a balance between witnesses from East and West in order to underline the truly catholic character of the *Catechism*. We also tried to take due account of the words of holy women.

The catechetical character of the book appears most clearly in the brief statements found at the end of each thematic unit. The *Catechism* itself says that their aim is to suggest to local catechesis brief summary formulae that could be memorized.[2]

Even a partially complete presentation of the *Catechism* would have to say a great deal further. It would have to touch, for example, upon ecumenism,[3] the *Catechism*'s relation to local catechisms and concrete catechetical work, and more besides. But I do not aspire to completeness here; my aim is simply to create a willingness to read the *Catechism* fairmindedly and to offer assistance in making the first step toward doing so. In conclusion I would like to cite the final words of the introduction to the *Catechism*, where it quotes from the foreword to the Catechism of the Council of Trent:

> The whole concern of doctrine and its teaching must be directed to the love that never ends. Whether something

[2] CCC 22.

[3] Unfortunately, a superficial and hasty reading of the text has given currency to numerous erroneous judgments about this important question. It has been remarked, for example, that the word "ecumenism" appears only once in the index. But this only shows how little a book can be explained by its index alone. From beginning to end the *Catechism* is, among other things, a dialogue with all the other Christian traditions. Worthwhile reading as an Orthodox reaction is T. Nikolau's article, "Gemeinsame altkirchliche Traditionen stärker berücksichtigen. Der Katechismus der katholischen Kirche aus orthodoxer Sicht", *KNA Ökumenische Information*, no. 19 (May 1994): 5–14.

is proposed for belief, for hope or for action, the love of our Lord must always be made accessible, so that anyone can see that all the works of perfect Christian virtue spring from love and have no other objective than to arrive at love.[4]

---

[4] CCC 25; *Roman Catechism*, preface, 10.

On the Meaning of Faith

Let me begin with a brief story from the early postconciliar period. The Council documents—particularly the Constitution on the Church in the Modern World, but also the decrees on ecumenism, on mission, on non-Christian religions, and on freedom of religion—had opened up broad vistas of dialogue for the Church and theology. New issues were appearing on the horizon, and it was becoming necessary to find new methods. It seemed self-evident that a theologian who wanted to be up to date and who rightly understood his task should temporarily suspend the old discussions and devote all of his energies to the new questions pressing in from every side.

At about this time, I sent a small piece of mine to Hans Urs von Balthasar. Balthasar replied by return mail on a correspondence card, as he always did, and, after expressing his thanks, added a terse sentence that made an indelible impression on me: Do not presuppose the faith but propose it. This was an imperative that hit home. Wide-ranging exploration of new fields was good and necessary, but only so long as it issued from, and was sustained by, the central light of faith. Faith is not maintained automatically. It is not a "finished business" that we can simply take for granted. The life of faith has to be constantly renewed. And

since faith is an act that comprehends all the dimen-
sions of our existence, it also requires constantly renewed reflection and witness. It follows that the chief
points of faith—God, Christ, the Holy Spirit, grace
and sin, sacraments and Church, death and eternal life
—are never outmoded. They are always the issues that
affect us most profoundly. They must be the permanent
center of preaching and therefore of theological reflection. The bishops present at the 1985 Synod called
for a universal catechism of the whole Church because
they sensed precisely what Balthasar had put into words
in his note to me. Their experience as shepherds had
shown them that the various new pastoral activities
have no solid basis unless they are irradiations and ap-
plications of the message of faith. Faith cannot be presupposed; it must be proposed. This is the purpose of
the *Catechism*. It aims to propose the faith in its fullness
and wealth, but also in its unity and simplicity.

What does the Church believe? This question implies
another: Who believes, and how does someone believe?
The *Catechism* treats these two main questions, which
concern, respectively, the "what" and the "who" of
faith, as an intrinsic unity. Expressed in other terms,
the *Catechism* displays the act of faith and the content
of faith in their indivisible unity. This may sound somewhat abstract, so let us try to unfold a bit what it means.
    We find in the creeds two formulas: "I believe" and
"We believe." We speak of the faith of the Church,

of the personal character of faith and finally of faith as a gift of God, as a "theological act", as contemporary theology likes to put it. What does all of this mean?

Faith is an orientation of our existence as a whole. It is a fundamental option that affects every domain of our existence. Nor can it be realized unless all the energies of our existence go into maintaining it. Faith is not a merely intellectual, or merely volitional, or merely emotional activity—it is all of these things together. It is an act of the whole self, of the whole person in his concentrated unity. The Bible describes faith in this sense as an act of the "heart" (Rom 10:9).

Faith is a supremely personal act. But precisely because it is supremely personal, it transcends the self, the limits of the individual. Augustine remarks that nothing is so little ours as our self. Where man as a whole comes into play, he transcends himself; an act of the whole self is at the same time always an opening to others, hence, an act of being together with others [*Mitsein*]. What is more, we cannot perform this act without touching our deepest ground, the living God who is present in the depths of our existence as its sustaining foundation.

Any act that involves the whole man also involves, not just the self, but the we-dimension, indeed, the wholly other "Thou", God, together with the self. But this also means that such an act transcends the reach of what I can do alone. Since man is a created being, the deepest truth about him is never just action but always passion as well; man is not only a giver but also a re-

ceiver. The *Catechism* expresses this point in the following words: "No one can believe alone, just as no
one can live alone. You have not given yourself faith
as you have not given yourself life."[1] Paul's description
of his experience of conversion and baptism alludes to
faith's radical character: "It is no longer I who live, but
Christ lives in me" (Gal 2:20). Faith is a perishing of
the mere self and precisely thus a resurrection of the
true self. To believe is to become oneself through liberation from the mere self, a liberation that brings us
into communion with God mediated by communion
with Christ.

So far, we have attempted, with the help of the *Catechism*, to analyze "who" believes, hence, to identify
the structure of the act of faith. But in so doing we
have already caught sight of the outlines of the essential content of faith. In its core, Christian faith is an
encounter with the living God. God is, in the proper
and ultimate sense, the content of our faith. Looked at
in this way, the content of faith is absolutely simple:
I believe in God. But this absolute simplicity is also
absolutely deep and encompassing. We can believe in
God because he can touch us, because he is in us, and
because he also comes to us from the outside. We can
believe in him because of the one whom he has sent.
"Because he has 'seen the Father,' " says the *Catechism*,

[1] CCC 166.

referring to John 6:56, "Jesus Christ is the only one who knows him and can reveal him."[2] We could say that to believe is to be granted a share in Jesus' vision. He lets us see with him in faith what he has seen.

This statement implies both the divinity of Jesus Christ and his humanity. Because Jesus is the Son, he has an unceasing vision of the Father. Because he is man, we can share this vision. Because he is both God and man at once, he is neither merely a historical person nor simply removed from all time in eternity. Rather, he is in the midst of time, always alive, always present.

But in saying this, we also touch upon the mystery of the Trinity. The Lord becomes present to us through the Holy Spirit. Let us listen once more to the *Catechism*: "One cannot believe in Jesus Christ without sharing in his Spirit. . . . Only God knows God completely: we believe *in* the Holy Spirit because he is God."[3]

It follows from what we have said that, when we see the act of faith correctly, the single articles of faith unfold by themselves. God becomes concrete for us in Christ. This has two consequences. On the one hand, the triune mystery of God becomes discernible; on the other hand, we see that God has involved himself in history to the point that the Son has become man and now sends us the Spirit from the Father. But the In-

[2] CCC 151.
[3] CCC 152.

carnation also includes the mystery of the Church, for Christ came to "gather into one the children of God who are scattered abroad" (Jn 11:52). The "we" of the Church is the new communion into which God draws us beyond our narrow selves (cf. Jn 12:32). The Church is thus contained in the first movement of the act of faith itself. The Church is not an institution extrinsically added to faith as an organizational framework for the common activities of believers. No, she is integral to the act of faith itself. The "I believe" is always also a "We believe." As the *Catechism* says, " 'I believe' is also the Church, our mother, responding to God by faith as she teaches us to say both 'I believe' and 'We believe.' "[4]

We observed just now that the analysis of the act of faith immediately displays faith's essential content as well: faith is a response to the triune God, the Father, the Son and the Holy Spirit. We can now add that the same act of faith also embraces God's incarnation in Jesus Christ, his theandric mystery, and thus the entirety of salvation history. It further becomes clear that the People of God, the Church as the human protagonist of salvation history, is present in the very act of faith. It would not be difficult to demonstrate in a similar fashion that the other items of belief are also explications of the one fundamental act of encountering

[4] CCC 167.

the living God. For by its very nature, relation to God has to do with eternal life. And this relation necessarily transcends the merely human sphere. God is truly God only if he is the Lord of all things. And he is the Lord of all things only if he is their Creator. Creation, salvation history and eternal life are thus themes that flow directly from the question of God. In addition, when we speak of God's history with man, we also imply the issue of sin and grace. We touch upon the question of how we encounter God, hence, the question of the liturgy, of the sacraments, of prayer and morality. But I do not want to develop all of these points in detail now; my chief concern has been precisely to get a glimpse of the intrinsic unity of faith, which is not a multitude of propositions but a full and simple act whose simplicity contains the whole depth and breadth of being. He who speaks of God, speaks of the whole; he learns to discern the essential from the inessential, and he comes to know, albeit only fragmentarily and "in a glass, darkly" (1 Cor 13:12) as long as faith is faith and not yet vision, something of the inner logic and unity of all reality.

Finally, I would like to touch briefly on the question we mentioned at the beginning of our reflections. I mean the question of *how* we believe. Paul furnishes us with a remarkable and extremely helpful statement on this matter when he says that faith is an obedience "from the heart to the form of doctrine into which

you were handed over" (Rom 6:17). These words ultimately express the sacramental character of faith, the intrinsic connection between confession and sacrament.
The Apostle says that a "form of doctrine" is an essential component of faith. We do not think up faith on
our own. It does not come *from* us as an idea of ours
but *to* us as a word from outside. It is, as it were, a
word about the Word; we are "handed over" *into* this
Word that reveals new paths to our reason and gives
form to our life.

We are "handed over" into the Word that precedes
us through an immersion in water symbolizing death.
This recalls the words of Paul cited earlier: "I live, yet
not I"; it reminds us that what takes place in the act
of faith is the destruction and renewal of the self. Baptism as a symbolic death links this renewal to the death
and Resurrection of Jesus Christ. To be handed over
into the doctrine is to be handed over into Christ.
We cannot receive his word as a theory in the same
way that we learn, say, mathematical formulas or philosophical opinions. We can learn it only in accepting
a share in Christ's destiny. But we can become shar-
ers in Christ's destiny only where he has permanently
committed himself to sharing in man's destiny: in the
Church. In the language of this Church we call this
event a "sacrament". The act of faith is unthinkable
without the sacramental component.

These remarks enable us to understand the concrete literary structure of the *Catechism*. To believe, as we have heard, is to be handed over into a form of doctrine. In another passage, Paul calls this form of doctrine a confession (cf. Rom 10:9). A further aspect of the faith-event thus emerges. That is, the faith that comes to us as a word must also become a word in us, a word that is simultaneously the expression of our life. To believe is always also to confess the faith. Faith is not private but something public that concerns the community. The word of faith first enters the mind, but it cannot stay there: thought must always become word and deed again.

The *Catechism* refers to the various kinds of confessions of faith that exist in the Church: baptismal confessions, conciliar confessions, confessions formulated by popes.[5] Each of these confessions has a significance of its own. But the primordial type that serves as a basis for all further developments is the baptismal creed. When we talk about catechesis, that is, initiation into the faith and adaptation of our existence to the Church's communion of faith, we must begin with the baptismal creed. This has been true since apostolic times and therefore imposed itself as the method of the *Catechism*, which, in fact, unfolds the contents of faith from the baptismal creed. It thus becomes appar-

[5] Cf. CCC 192.

ent how the *Catechism* intends to teach the faith: catechesis is catechumenate. It is not merely religious instruction but the act whereby we surrender ourselves
and are received *into* the word of faith and communion
with Jesus Christ. Adaptation to God's ways is an essential part of catechesis. Saint Irenaeus says a propos
of this that we must accustom ourselves to God, just
as in the Incarnation God accustomed himself to us
men. We must accustom ourselves to God's ways so
that we can learn to bear his presence in us. Expressed
in theological terms, this means that the image of God
—which is what makes us capable of communion of
life with him—must be freed from its encasement of
dross. The tradition compares this liberation to the activity of the sculptor who chisels away at the stone bit
by bit until the form that he beholds emerges into visi-
bility.

Catechesis should always be such a process of assimilation to God. After all, we can only know a reality if
there is something in us corresponding to it. Goethe,
alluding to Plotinus, says that "the eye could never
recognize the sun were it not itself sunlike."[6] The cog-
nitional process is a process of assimilation, a vital process. The "we", the "what" and the "how" of faith belong together.

This brings to light the moral dimension of the act

[6] "Wär nicht das Auge sonnenhaft, die Sonne könnt' es nicht er-
kennen."

of faith, which includes a style of humanity we do not produce by ourselves but that we gradually learn by plunging into our baptismal existence. The sacrament of penance is one such immersion into baptism, in which God again and again acts on us and draws us back to himself. Morality is an integral component of Christianity, but this morality is always part of the sacramental event of "Christianization" [*Christwerdung*] —an event in which we are not the sole agents but are always, indeed, primarily, receivers. And this reception entails transformation.

The *Catechism* therefore cannot be accused of any fanciful attachment to the past when it unfolds the contents of faith using the baptismal creed of the Church of Rome, the so-called "Apostles' Creed". Rather, this option brings to the fore the authentic core of the act of faith and thus of catechesis as existential training in existence with God.

Equally apparent is that the *Catechism* is wholly structured according to the principle of the hierarchy of truths as understood by the Second Vatican Council. For, as we have seen, the creed is in the first instance a confession of faith in the triune God developed from, and bound to, the baptismal formula. All of the "truths of faith" are explications of the *one* truth that we discover in them. And this one truth is the pearl of great price that is worth staking our lives on: God. He alone can be the pearl for which we give everything else. *Dios solo basta*[7]—he who finds God has found all things. But we can find him only because he has first sought and found us. He is the one who acts first, and for this reason faith in God is inseparable from the mystery of the Incarnation, of the Church and of the sacraments. Everything that is said in the *Catechism* is an unfolding of the one truth that is God himself—the "love that moves the sun and all the stars".[8]

[7] "God alone suffices."—TRANS.
[8] Dante, *Paradiso* 33, 145.

Evangelization,
Catechesis and Catechism

Since the episcopal Synods of 1974 and 1977, two ancient biblical words have come, first almost inconspicuously, then with steadily growing intensity, to the foreground of the Church's consciousness: evangelization and catechization.

The origin of the first term makes it particularly inflammatory, nor has it failed to ignite controversy. "Evangelization" is suspected of being a code word for an attempted Catholic restoration that clings nostalgically to the dream of the old Catholic Europe and aims to reestablish the hegemony of Catholic faith and thought. But believers throughout the world hear the word differently. For them, it refers purely to the hope-generating power of Jesus' message, whose historical novelty and specificity are expressed in a concentrated form in the term "gospel" (cf. Mk 1:1; 1:15).[1]

---

[1] The German text has *Evangelium*, a word that remains close in form to the original Greek *evangelion*, meaning "good news". *Evangelium* also shares a common root with two other German words, *evangelisieren*, "evangelize", and *Evangelisierung*, "evangelization", that appear frequently in this chapter. The author occasionally uses *Evangelium* together with one or both of these derivatives. This allows a terminological coherence that is lost when *Evangelium* is rendered with "gospel" (the word "evangel" exists in English but sounds somewhat outlandish). However, the reader should bear in mind that

The insights and instructions that gradually took shape among the bishops gathered for discussion at the 1974 Synod are summed up in one of the most beautiful post-conciliar documents, the apostolic exhortation drafted by Paul VI under the title *Evangelii nuntiandi*. The next Synod examined one important aspect of evangelization, namely, catechesis, in greater detail. The current Pope presented the results of this Synod to the Church and the world in the constitution *Catechesi tradendæ*. The same impulse that led the bishops to underscore evangelization and catechesis as the focal points of contemporary pastoral ministry in the seventies would prompt the call for a common catechism of the whole Catholic Church at the Synod of 1985. This book, which appeared exactly thirty years after the inauguration of the Council, can be understood only if we keep in mind the efforts of the 1970s to give concrete shape to the evangelization and catechization that Vatican II had called for.

It is no surprise that the *Catechism* proved to be a sign of contradiction from its very inception, even before anyone had read a single line of it. This only goes to show the timeliness of a work that is not merely a book but an event in the history of the Church. Anything that does not meet with opposition has obviously not

---

"gospel" is itself a literal rendering of the Greek *evangelion* composed of the Anglo-Saxon words for "good" and "news".—TRANS.

dealt at all with the urgent needs of its time. The worst thing that Christianity has experienced in the twentieth century has not been open antagonism. The fact that powerful regimes persecute a powerless minority of believers with every means at their disposal is a sign of how much inner strength they attribute to the faith that animates this little flock. What *is* oppressive, however, is indifference toward Christianity, which is apparently no longer worth a struggle but is regarded as an insignificant antique that we can safely let go to ruin, or even maintain as a museum piece. In contrast, the *Catechism* was and is an event that has reached far beyond intra-ecclesial debates to stir a secularized society. The *Catechism* was and is a breach in the soundproof walls of indifference. Faith is once more becoming salt that wounds and heals, a summons that challenges us to take a position.

Before we ask what function the *Catechism* can exercise in the context of the fundamental task of evangelization and catechization, we must try to explain briefly the content of these two terms in themselves. When we inquire into the biblical roots of the two words, as it befits Christian theology to do, we discover the important fact that both are specifically Christian terms, which as such first took shape in the writings of the New Testament. The Greek word for gospel is a striking illustration of this. Rabbinic literature transcribes the Greek loan word *evangelion* into Hebrew letters,

38   *Gospel, Catechesis, Catechism*

precisely in order to characterize the message of the
Christians.[2] When it comes to the word "catechize",
the historical evidence is in many respects even clearer,
for the word does not occur at all in the Greek translation of the Old Testament, the Septuagint; Paul was
the first one to give it its specific and permanent significance.[3] We thus find ourselves before realities that
bring home to us the novelty and specificity of Christianity.

1. The Significance of the Terms "Gospel" and "Evangelize" in the Light of the Bible and the Catechism

Let us begin by examining somewhat more closely
the word "gospel" (evangelize, and so on). As we
have just said, it was Jesus' activity that first conferred
upon this word its specific sense. Nevertheless, the
term builds on two pre-Christian foundations, which
are then welded together and given a new meaning in
the gospel of Jesus.

The first element is the message of joy in Deutero-
Isaiah: glad tidings are brought to the poor (Is 58:6;
61:1). The word "the poor" as used here is already
beginning to designate the faithful Israel that suffers

---

[2] G. Friedrich, "*euangelizomai*", *ThWNT* 2:705–35; on this point,
see 723f.

[3] H. W. Beyer 3:*ThWNT*, 3:638–40.

for God's sake and has stood fast through all the catastrophes of history precisely in the person of the simple and the poor.

Alongside this Old Testament root is a non-Jewish one, a sort of political theology typical of the great kingdoms of the Orient, of the Hellenistic kingdoms and finally of the Roman *Imperium*. In this context, "gospel" means the news of a new ruler's accession to the throne. His actions are "glad tidings". He ushers in—this is the constant refrain of the proclamation —a new and better time; he gives peace, justice and well-being; his existence and action are "gospel", a renewal of the world and of history.[4] In short, the term is an assertion that utopia has been realized, and in this sense it is reminiscent of this century's utopian gospels of salvation, with their announcement of a new man and a new society.

The gospel of Jesus Christ radically transforms this political theology. The new "kingdom" comes, not from this or that ruler, this or that ideology, but only from God himself. But we come to God in communion with the crucified and risen Jesus of Nazareth. This brings us to the new Christian meaning of the word "gospel", which we can present in the following three stages.

[4] Cf. Friedrich, *"euangelizomai"*, 705–7; 721f.

a. Jesus' Gospel

The first layer is Jesus' own proclamation of the gospel
as transmitted by the evangelists. From the very outset
Jesus' preaching indissolubly links the terms "gospel"
and "kingdom of God" (kingdom of heaven, reign of
God).[5] The kingdom of God is God himself. When
Jesus says "the kingdom of God is near", he first means
simply that God himself is near. You are near God, he is
near you. Jesus also means that God is a God who acts.
God is not exiled in the "transcendental" sphere that
supposedly separates him from the "categorial" sphere
in which we act and live. He is present, and he has
power. Though seemingly absent and impotent, God is
the only one who is truly present and truly reigns—
differently, to be sure, from what either human poten-
tates or powerless yet power-hungry men imagine.

In this sense, Jesus' message is altogether simple; it
is a message about the God who is present and who
lives within calling distance from us.[6] In what follows,
we will have to reflect on what actually constitutes
the novelty of Jesus' message. First, however, I think
it would already be good to pause and take stock of

[5] Mk 1:15.

[6] Concerning Jesus' concept of the kingdom of God, I would like
to draw particular attention to the thorough presentation in P. Stuhlmacher's *Biblische Theologie des Neuen Testaments, I: Grundlegung. Von
Jesus zu Paulus* (Göttingen, 1992), 66–75. Cf. also J. Gnilka, *Jesus von
Nazareth* (Freiburg, 1990), 87–165. The *Catechism* devotes sections
541–60 to Jesus' proclamation of the kingdom of God.

our attitude to this core of Jesus' proclamation. What role does God really play in our preaching? Do we not normally avoid the issue and shift to matters that we deem more "concrete" and more urgent—to political, social, economic and psychological questions, to questions of Church reform and criticism? We think that everyone knows about God already, that the subject of "God" has little to say to our everyday problems. Jesus corrects us: God is *the* practical, *the* realistic topic for man—in Jesus' time and in every time. As disciples of Jesus Christ, we have to give men what they most need—communion with the living God. Are we not all infected to varying degrees with an unacknowledged deism?[7] We think that God is too far away, that he does not reach into our daily life; so, we say to ourselves, let's speak of close-at-hand, practical realities. No, says Jesus: God is present, he is within call. This is the first word of the gospel, which changes our whole life when we put our faith in it. This has to be said to our world with completely new vigor on the authority of Christ.

However, we must pay still closer attention to the few texts in which the term "gospel" occurs in the mouth of Jesus himself. It is typical in these texts, first of all, for the gospel (in the tradition of Isaiah) to be intended primarily for the poor (Lk 4:18). Linked to this first characteristic are deeds of salvation and heal-

---

[7] For a helpful analysis of this deism that is secretly present even in theology, see H. Jonas, *Macht oder Ohnmacht der Subjektivität?* (Frankfurt am Main, 1981).

ing: the blind see, the lame walk, lepers are cleansed, the deaf speak, and the dead are raised (Mt 11:5; Lk 7:22). The gospel is not just a matter of words but also of deeds. In the gospel, God shows himself as one who acts. He acts on behalf of those who need him most and await him with an open heart, confident that he will and can save them. The *Catechism* says it beautifully:

> The kingdom belongs *to the poor and lowly*, which means those who have accepted it with humble hearts. . . . Jesus shares the life of the poor, from the cradle to the cross. . . . Jesus identifies himself with the poor of every kind and makes active love toward them the condition for entering his kingdom.[8]

In this passage, the *Catechism* points to the deepest root of what today we call the "preferential option for the poor". It is evident that we Christians cannot choose or decline this option at our discretion. Rather, it is a requirement flowing from the essential core of the gospel itself.[9]

Jesus' life is the best interpretation of the motive and meaning of the option for the poor. Christ, the Son of David, does not come into the world in a royal palace, as the Magi expect, but in a manger. His first public

[8] CCC 544; cf. 559.

[9] Cf. the Santo Domingo document of the Latin American bishops: *New Evangelization—Promotion of Man—Christian Culture.*

and official designation as "king" is the title of execution placed above his head on the Cross. His disciples
are fishermen—not erudite theologians, but representatives of the simple folk.

Yet another fact, which is nonetheless connected
with what we have just seen, emerges when we hear
Jesus' declaration that he has come "to seek and to save
what was lost" (Lk 19:10). This so to say "shorthand"
summary already reveals something of the many-faceted
option for the poor carried in the Incarnation of the
Son of God. The meaning of this option comes perhaps most clearly to light in Jesus' words about children: "Unless you turn and become like children, you
will never enter the kingdom of heaven. Whosoever
humbles himself like this child, he is the greatest in
the kingdom of heaven" (Mt 18:3−4). This saying is a
particularly compact expression of a whole theology of
littleness, of the little ones, and of childhood that we
find in Jesus. It ultimately has—like this entire series of
words—a christological content pointing to the inner
biography of Jesus himself. It is Jesus who became totally small, who is "littler", for example, than John the
Baptist (Mt 11:11). Jesus is entirely "Son" and is never
enclosed in his own world. He is, with every fiber of
his existence, relation to the Father.

Why is this so? This far-reaching question, which concerns nothing less than the characteristic shape of God's
dealings with man, can be answered only in outline

here. I think we can discover two profound reasons for this direction of God's action, which is meant to show man how to direct his action.

First of all, we can speak of God's "compassion". God hears the cry of the oppressed and afflicted of this world. It is this cry that stirs his heart and constrains him to come down to us. God "hears" even when men become mute by falling into sin and, with that, into the direst poverty of all—loss of truth, of love, of God. Because God is the Creator, he loves all creatures. God's own nature—love—compels him to meet these manifold and diverse, even contrary, kinds of need. Indeed, it even constrains him to enter into them in order to change them from within. "You therefore must be perfect as your heavenly Father is perfect" (Mt 5:48) —in the light of what we have just said, this staggering conclusion of the Sermon on the Mount means: Be infected by the dynamism of a love that cannot abide in the glory of heaven while the cry of the suffering rises up from the earth. A bishop recently told me that on the day of his first Mass his father said to him: "I would rather see you die than become hard-hearted." This is precisely the point here. In the end, evangelization means to set out with Christ in order to pass on the gift we have received, to transform poverty of every kind.

This is connected to the second motif, which we recognize in the Son's poverty and in his concern for the poor of every description. Jesus' poverty establishes criteria for us. Power and possession are not evil as such, nor are they to be rejected as a matter of principle. To a certain extent, they are even necessary. However, they are not an end in themselves but a means that not only imposes on man an increased responsibility but also involves an increased risk for him. Precisely the one to whom power is entrusted must know that he does not have it of and for himself, that it is conferred upon him for the sake of service and that he must stand before God as a poor man who is judged on the honesty and humility of his service. He has nothing but what he has done for others in his servant's responsibility. The same is true for the rich man. He too will stand before God as a poor man, and he will be rich only to the extent that his possessions have become a means of service and love. Finally, this line of thought is also given expression in the Lord's words, "I thank thee, Father, Lord of heaven and earth, that thou hast hidden these things from the wise and understanding and revealed them to babes" (Mt 11:25). Education and knowledge can be a blessing only when that deeper simplicity of heart —that inward poverty (Mt 5:3!) that can hear God's word and obey it in humble faith—remains in place. This "wealth" is also a responsibility to serve. Whenever it fails to become "evangelization" of the poor, it withdraws into a self-sufficiency forgetful of its own neediness. It is precisely in this way that it causes us to lose our soul (cf. Mt 10:39).

Let us return to Jesus' proclamation of the kingdom of
God, that is, to his gospel. A further dimension that
we must now consider is that this proclamation occurs
in the horizon of judgment and promise, of responsibility and hope. Man is not free to do or not do what
he pleases. He is judged. He must render an account.
This conviction applies no less to the powerful than to
the simple. When this conviction is respected, worldly
power is kept within bounds. *God* creates justice, and,
in the end, only he can do it. We will be more suc-
cessful in establishing justice the more we live under
God's eyes and are able to communicate to the world
the truth of judgment. The judgment, together with
its conscience-forming power, is a central point of the
gospel.[10] It is glad tidings, good news for all who suffer injustice in this world and are in search of justice.
Once again, we perceive the connection between the
kingdom of God and the "poor", the suffering and all
those spoken of in the Beatitudes. Only when we have
inwardly accepted judgment and the resulting seriousness of our responsibility do we also understand the
other element that is present in Jesus' life and that finds
its most profound expression in the Cross, namely, that
"God is greater than our heart" (1 Jn 3:20). The invitation of "sinners to the table of the kingdom" spo-

---

[10] Cf. M. Reiser, *Die Gerichtspredigt Jesu. Eine Untersuchung zur escha-
tologischen Verkündigung Jesu und ihrem frühjüdischen Hintergrund* (Munich, 1990).

ken of in the *Catechism*[11] does not abolish judgment or thin down God's goodness to a syrupy sentimentality devoid of truth. It first becomes a redeeming message only for those who believe in God's righteous judgment.

So far we have seen that the gospel Jesus preached is a rigorously theocentric message that makes God himself present and logically entails a certain interpretation of man in the world. When we listen to the relevant sections of the *Catechism* (541–50), we can see that Jesus' own words already contain a further layer that in turn serves as the bridge to the nascent Church's concept of "gospel".

Earlier Catholic exegesis often almost completely identified the kingdom of God and the Church, which it liked to describe as the "kingdom of God on earth". In contrast, liberal and postliberal exegesis—taking its cue especially from Johannes Weiß and Albert Schweitzer—formed a strictly eschatological conception of the kingdom of God. It saw the term as an expression of Jesus' expectation of the imminent end of the world and of the coming world of God. Beginning in the 1920s, even Catholic exegesis increasingly adopted this perspective. More recently, the "kingdom"—in a secularizing variation on this idea (which cannot be assimilated into Catholic theology)—became

[11] CCC 545.

an expression for the expectation of the better world to
be established by the concerted effort of the religions.
This amounted, however, to a dismissal of Jesus' message itself. Meanwhile, scientific exegesis has largely
dropped the purely eschatological interpretation of the
message of the kingdom of God and is pushing more
and more toward a properly christological interpretation of this central term in Jesus' preaching.

Recently, Peter Stuhlmacher has convincingly shown
the close connection between the kingdom of God and
Jesus' awareness of his divine sonship. Only at this
point does the truly new and revolutionary element
in Jesus' message about the kingdom come to the fore.
Jesus does not simply preach God's presence and power
in general; God is now present and near in a much more
radical way. He is present in Jesus himself. The Son is
the kingdom. Stuhlmacher says on this point: "In at-
testing to and teaching the gospel of God's reign, Jesus
is the Son who acts and teaches in the name of the
Father." [12]

This discovery also permits a fresh reading of Jesus'
parables. The parables, like the message of the kingdom, were earlier understood in a predominantly ec-

[12] Stuhlmacher, *Biblische Theologie*, 75. On p. 74, Stuhlmacher points
out that Jesus' claim that God is immediately present in his words and
deeds explodes the limits hitherto set by the Torah and the liturgical
assembly and that this process represents the beginnings of Jesus' Passion. The message of the kingdom and the mystery of Easter go together. The following chapter on Israel, the Church and the world
attempts to unfold this connection more clearly.

clesiological key, then for the most part in a strictly eschatological sense. It was said that the parables must not be interpreted as allegories. This was a way of saying that the individual features of the narrative were not significant; all that mattered was the main point, which was almost universally regarded as the proclamation of the sudden coming of the wholly Other. Today a growing number of exegetes realize that in the parables Jesus is speaking of himself, explaining the mystery of his mission and thus the mystery of the kingdom. On this point the *Catechism* says the following:

> Jesus and the presence of the kingdom in this world are secretly at the heart of the parables. One must enter the kingdom, that is, become a disciple of Christ, in order to 'know the secrets of the kingdom of heaven' [Mt 13:11]. For those who stay 'outside,' everything remains enigmatic. [13]

All the parables contain an indirect Christology; they speak "in code" about Christ and therefore about the kingdom that is now entering the world. This is quite obvious in the case of some parables. Examples would be the parable of the wicked vintners (Mt 12:1–12), which Jesus develops from the prophetic tradition, or else his saying about the old and new wine (Mk 2:18–22). In other parables—such as those of the seed, of the wedding feast, of the salt and of the light—the figure of Jesus remains more in the background. Neverthe-

[13] CCC 546.

less, it can be discerned by the attentive reader, especially if he takes account of the events that form the
context of the respective parable. This context is an
altogether indispensable aid for finding the key to the
parables. The parables belong with the events; they are
not merely addressed to hearers and thinkers but lead us
into that event which, in the end, is the theme of all the
parables—entry into the kingdom of God that comes
with Jesus. In this sense, they make a totally concrete
claim: they are invitations to discipleship. In order to
understand these parables, we must share Christ's existence. Their meaning is inaccessible to anyone who
attempts to lay hold of them in a merely intellectual-
historical or speculative way. "To those who remain
outside, the whole remains a parable, so that seeing they
may not see and hearing not understand . . ." (cf. Mk
4:11–12).[14]

Jesus' proclamation was never mere preaching, mere
words; it was "sacramental", in the sense that his
words were and are inseparable from his "I"—from
his "flesh". His word opens up only in the context of
the signs he performed, of his life and of his death. *The*
sign—the culminating point of his life that reveals the
center of his "I"—is the Paschal Mystery. The *Cate-*
chism says here that "above all in the great Paschal mystery—his death on the cross and his Resurrection—he
would accomplish the coming of his kingdom. 'And I,

[14] CCC 541.

when I am lifted up from the earth, will draw all men to myself'. [Jn 12:32]"[15] He himself is the kingdom, he is the nearness of God to and with us of which we have spoken. The center of Jesus' figure [*Gestalt*] is thus his death and his Resurrection. In these events, God's kingdom comes, ever anew.[16]

b. The Gospel in the Gospels

The Christology implicit in Jesus' proclamation of the gospel through his speech, action and suffering was subsequently made explicit by the Church in the light of the Easter event. The Holy Spirit who came on Pentecost led the disciples into all truth (cf. Jn 16:13). In their constant meditation and reflection upon Jesus' parables, words and deeds, the disciples discovered that the Paschal Mystery had been at the center of Jesus' whole proclamation. To call the four accounts of Matthew, Mark, Luke and John "Gospels" is precisely to express that Jesus himself, the entirety of his acting, teaching, living, rising and remaining with us is the "gospel". The four basic texts of the New Testament are not simply books but the written record of a proclamation. Since Easter, the method of evangelization has been to tell men what we now read in the Gospels. In saying

[15] CCC 542.

[16] The *Catechism* thereby adopts in a certain sense the position of C. H. Dodd (*The Founder of Christianity*), without taking over its one-sided judgments.

this, we do not mean to retract any of what we have
just discovered to be the content of Jesus' proclamation
of the Gospel. Only through the four Gospels do we
know this gospel. It must be constantly retold in all its
freshness and explosive power. But we would not tell
the whole gospel if we were to leave out the Person
through whom the word has become a reality for us.
We proclaim Jesus' message in its integrity only when
we proclaim Jesus himself. He is God's being with us.
Through him God is truly an acting subject in history.
In him God's will is wholly fulfilled, and where God's
will is fulfilled, there is "heaven".

There is, then, no discontinuity between Jesus' pre-
Easter message and the message preached by the disciples after Easter and Pentecost. We cannot say that Jesus
spoke of the kingdom of God, the apostles proclaimed
Christ instead, and the Church finished the process by
putting herself at the center. Jesus was much more than
a rather headstrong rabbi, nor was he anything at all like
a zealot fomenting revolution against Roman rule. We
could say that Jesus was a surprise, a figure no one had
expected to come in just the way he did.[17] Only in
the light of Easter, in the light of the Holy Spirit, did

[17] V. Messori persuasively demonstrates that the figure of Jesus
could not have been deduced from existing expectations of salvation
that took their direction from the Old Testament: *Patì sotto Ponzio Pilato?* (Turin, 1992), 230–39. Only a new, Paschal reading could enable believers to realize that Moses and the prophets had spoken of
Jesus.

believers gradually come to understand that Moses and the prophets had in fact spoken of Jesus, just as the two disciples realized this truth while Jesus walked and talked with them on the road to Emmaus. After their hearts had burned within them, their eyes were finally opened, and "they knew him" (Lk 24:31). We could thus say—and this is our second layer—that to evangelize means to acquaint men with Jesus as we come to know him through the Gospels. To evangelize is to introduce men into a communion of life with him as well as into the fellowship of disciples, the community that journeys with him.

c. Paul's Gospel

We find in Paul, at a deeper level still, yet another way of using the term "gospel". Paul speaks of "my gospel", whereby he expresses the special insight given to him in his encounter with the risen Christ on the road to Damascus, namely, that man is not justified before God by the works of the law but by faith. We could briefly state the core of Saint Paul's intuition in something like the following words. In order to enter into God's will, in order to live his will, I do not have to become a Jewish proselyte; I do not need to submit to the mass of prescriptions contained in the Torah. It suffices to convert to Jesus and to live in communion with him.

The connection between this insight and the message of the kingdom of God becomes plain when we listen

to the words of the prominent Jewish scholar Jacob
Neusner: "When I accept the yoke of the commandments of the Torah and do them, I accept God's rule.
I live in the kingdom of God, which is to say, in the
dominion of Heaven, here on earth. To lead a holy life
means to live here and now according to God's will."[18]
The Christian can agree entirely with Neusner; he need
only replace the word "Torah" with another word—
the name "Jesus". Instead of saying, "when I accept
the yoke of the commandments of the Torah and do
them . . . I am in the kingdom of God", the Christian will say, "when I am in communion with Jesus,
I live in the kingdom of God." Jesus is the Torah in
person; I have the whole of it when I have Jesus. This
substitution of the name Jesus for the word Torah is
Paul's "gospel"; it is the content of his doctrine of jus-
tification. Implicit in Paul's teaching is the revolution
of Christianity, inasmuch as it effectively universalizes
the people of God.[19]

New evangelization should thus take its inspiration
above all from Saint Paul's encounter with Christ. For
the capacity to free oneself in a positive and fruitful

[18] J. Neusner, *A Rabbi Talks with Jesus: An Intermillennial Interfaith Exchange* (New York, Doubleday: 1993), 19.

[19] On Paul's use of the word "gospel", see P. Stuhlmacher, *Das Paulinische Evangelium I* (1968); idem, *Das Evangelium und die Evangelien* (1983), esp. 157–82; idem, "Evangelium", *EKL* 1:1217–21; idem, *Biblische Theologie*, 312–26.

way from cultural pressures, from the "paradigms" of
an age; the capacity to become detached from cultural
embodiments of the faith and to be open to encounters
with new cultures—all of this depends upon this central experience: I must have met God in Christ in such
a living way that I can "count as dust" (Phil 3:7) my
own cultural provenance, indeed, everything that was
important to me in my own history. No studies, however subtle, will produce new cultural forms of Christianity unless they proceed from the liberating power
of encounter with Christ, the encounter in whose light
we can distinguish the "dust" from the "pearl" that is
worth giving everything to possess.

2. Catechesis, Catechization, Catechism

a. The Biblical Foundation and
Concept of Catechesis

So far, we have attempted to see and understand in
broad outline the meaning of the terms "gospel" and
"evangelization". We must now turn our attention to
the semantic field defined by "catechism" and "catechesis". The term "catechesis" takes second place to
"gospel", which remains the basic word. Catechesis
denotes a particular task that becomes necessary in the
context of evangelization. As I mentioned already at
the beginning, the word "catechesis" acquired its specific meaning in the language of Saint Paul; it is a term

that resulted from his apostolic activity. In addition, it also occurs here and there in Lukan theology. The most significant passage concerning catechesis is Galatians 6:6, which speaks of the catechumen and the catechist, hence, of the active and passive side of the process. In Acts, Luke describes Apollos as a man who is "catechized" in the way of the Lord (18:25); he dedicates his Gospel to Theophilus in order that the latter might come to know the trustworthiness of the words and realities (*logon*) in which he has been catechized.[20]

What does all this mean? We could say that while the four Gospels are evangelization, they also inaugurate the development of evangelization into catechesis. Catechesis aims at coming to know Jesus concretely. It is theoretical and practical initiation into the will of God as revealed in Jesus and lived by the community of the Lord's disciples, the family of God. On the one hand, the necessity of catechesis follows from the intellectual dimension of the gospel itself. The gospel addresses itself to reason; it responds to man's longing to understand the world and himself and to discover the way to do justice to his essential being. In this sense, catechesis is instruction, and the early Christian teachers were really the founders of the state of catechists in the Church. But the actual living out of this doctrine is an essential component of it, and man's intellect sees prop-

20 Cf. Beyer, *ThWNT* 3:638–40.

erly only when the heart is integrated into the mind. Consequently, catechetical instruction also includes a pilgrim fellowship, a gradual familiarization with the new life-style of Christianity. Very early on, this insight gave rise to the catechumenate, which aspired to provide that shared journey and conversation whose archetype is found in the disciples who walk with the risen Lord on the road to Emmaus.

Relying closely on the postsynodal document *Catechesi tradendæ*, the *Catechism* offers a definition of catechesis informed by the vision presented above. It is worth listening to this lovely text at somewhat greater length:

> "At the heart of catechesis we find, in essence, a Person, the Person of Jesus of Nazareth, the only Son from the Father. . . ." To catechize is "to reveal in the Person of Christ the whole of God's eternal design reaching fulfillment in that Person. . . ." Catechesis aims at putting "people . . . in communion . . . with Jesus Christ: only he can lead us to the love of the Father in the Spirit and make us share in the life of the Holy Trinity."[21]

> In catechesis, "Christ, the incarnate Word and Son of God, . . . is taught—everything else is taught with reference to him—and it is Christ alone who teaches—anyone else teaches to the extent that he is Christ's spokesman, enabling Christ to teach with his lips. . . . Every catechist should be able to apply to himself the

[21] CCC 426; *Catechesi tradendæ*, 5.

mysterious words of Jesus: 'My teaching is not mine, but his who sent me' [Jn 7:16]."[22]

b. The Context of the *Catechism*

The *Catechism* fits this conception of catechesis. It, too, has no other intention than to let Christ speak and to accompany catechumens in the process of assimilating their life and thought to the fellowship of Jesus Christ's disciples, who have become his family because they are united with him in the will of God (cf. Mk 3:34f.). This means, first of all, that the *Catechism* does not present the private theories of individual authors. This would be totally impossible if only because it is not the work of particular authors at all. In fact, the genesis of the *Catechism* brought together a flood of voices from the whole Church. None of those who worked on the *Catechism* in any of its numerous stages of redaction wanted to "put himself forward" but to make himself available to the communion of the Church as an ear and a mouth. This deprivatization of thought, this expropriation for the sake of the whole, proved to be a grand and gratifying experience. For everyone the law was, "my teaching is not mine." Theologians who peruse the *Catechism* only to see if their hypotheses have been accepted are obviously unaware of this. By the same token, both simple and cultured people on every continent are all the more sensitive to this fact. They

[22] CCC 427; *Catechesi tradendæ*, 6.

hear the voice of the Church and in it the voice of Jesus Christ. Meanwhile, they are rejoicing, as an abundance of letters from the whole world attests.

The whole tradition of the catechumenate in the Church makes it clear that the *Catechism*, as a book, is only *one* element in a larger whole.

On the one hand, the *Catechism* appeals to the "interior teacher" (to speak with Augustine) present in every man. This interior master enables every person who encounters Jesus' message to realize, "yes, this is it, this is what I have been looking for all along." On the other hand, the *Catechism* needs the exterior teacher, the catechist, as well as the companionship of the communion of disciples. Without the living words of the catechist who, like Apollos, is himself "catechized according to the way of the Lord" (Acts 18:25), the book remains dumb.

Catechists, acting in inward harmony with the faith of the Church, with the message of Jesus Christ, must creatively mediate the *Catechism* to given situations and persons. Even now, the *Catechism*, when it is not intentionally thwarted, is bringing forth an abundance of initiatives in evangelization and proclamation. But at the origin of these initiatives there is always the person of the catechist. When the Church has ceased to be something external for him but has "awakened in his soul", he can, with his dynamic faith, retransform the letter into a living voice. He will face contradiction, but above all he will evoke the joy that comes from meeting Jesus.

c. On the Didactic Structure of the *Catechism*

Finally, I would like to take a few moments to point out the didactic structure of the *Catechism*. When the synodal Fathers voted for a universal catechism in 1985, they stipulated that it must be biblical and liturgical and be written in the context of the situations in which contemporary man lives.

Now, these situations can be very diverse. There is little in common between the living conditions of a Swiss and a Bangladeshi (to take an example). Although the *Catechism* was written very much in a spirit of solidarity with the thought, life and even suffering of today's world, the work of relating it to real-life situations must be left to the creativity of the local churches and to the believing experience of the individual catechists and catechumens. For this reason, the *Catechism* is all the more at pains to think and speak in terms of the Bible and the liturgy. In Germany, however, the opposition to the *Catechism* appeals precisely to exegesis. The *Catechism* is portrayed as the work of yokels who have stubbornly refused to accept the findings of modern biblical exegesis. We shall address this particular point later. Independently of the question as to how modern the exegesis on which the *Catechism* relies may or may not be, an honest reader must admit without

cavil that the book is shaped from one end to the other
by the Bible. As far as I know, there has never been
until now a catechism so thoroughly formed by the
Bible. Even the German Bishops' Adult Catechism[23] is
not biblically informed to the same degree.

Long passages of the *Catechism* are narrative in character. The *Catechism* recounts the story of Jesus, the
story of God with us, as the Bible relates. This may
seem naïve to critical minds, but it was the catechetical
method of the apostles, if indeed we are justified in regarding the Gospels as a written record of the most ancient catechesis. It is the kind of catechesis that suggests
itself spontaneously when we believe what is written
and do not presume to know the history narrated better
than the sources. For the *Catechism*, the message of the
Bible is a reality, which as such can, in fact, must, be
told in this fashion even today.

The structure of the text always comprises three elements. The first is the "catechesis" proper, the presentation of the individual teachings of the faith. In
the second phase, the *Catechism* at once enlivens and
deepens this catechesis by introducing the choir of witnesses through representative texts of the great teachers
of the faith from every century. Naturally, the Church
Fathers, not to mention liturgical and magisterial texts,

[23] English edition: *The Church's Confession of Faith: A Catholic Catechism for Adults* (San Francisco: Ignatius Press, 1987).

have pride of place here. Note how much care was taken to give as equable as possible a hearing to the voices of the Eastern and Western Churches. In this way, the *Catechism* complements the synchronic element with the diachronic. The believers of all ages are permanent members of the living Church, nor do they ever simply fade into the past. In the selection of texts from the subsequent epochs of Church history, an effort was made to let the voices of the great women of the Church be heard.

There is also a tacit ecumenical dimension in all this. In drawing from the whole breadth of the tradition, the *Catechism* underscores what is essential and common while bringing into relief the manifold forms in which the faith is understood.

Finally, the short texts (called "In Brief") that conclude each section draw into relief the essential catechetical substance contained in the foregoing explanation. The *Catechism*'s ambition is not to replace this explanation with formulas that one day catechumens all over the world might learn by heart. Even within a single country the cultural and pedagogical circumstances vary so greatly that such an attempt could have no hope of success. What the *Catechism* does aim to do, however, is to offer elements for a common basic language of faith as well as for a renewal of the common memory of Christians. After all, as the one People of God, Christians are possessors of a common history.

The memory of God's deeds, which bind and gather us together, gives us a common identity as God's family, regardless of all differences. Part of this familial identity is the use of a common language, hence, the capacity to understand one another in the essentials. If the Church is to remain internally united, if men are to be able to live together in peace irrespective of all racial, political and cultural barriers, it is essential that faith not melt away into vagueness through a loss of memory and speech. Such faith would be ineffectual and empty. To be sure, it is not the task of catechesis to make us memorize a mass of texts. However, part of its task is a constant renewal and development of Christian memory and of the common understanding of the key words of the faith.

3. The Biblical Realism of the New Catechism's *Christological Catechesis*

So far we have spoken quite generally about the nature of evangelization and catechesis using the *Catechism* as our guide. We said at the outset that evangelization is the proclamation of God's nearness in word and deed together with instruction in his will through initiation into communion with Jesus Christ. And we have seen that catechesis develops the fundamental event of evangelization by familiarizing us with Jesus and that this takes place in the assimilation of our life and thought

to that of the community of disciples. The figure of
Jesus Christ is the center that links the two events of
"evangelization" and "catechesis". As a way of making all of these points more concrete, I would like to
devote this concluding section to illustrating how the
Catechism conceives of the catechetical task and in so
doing blazes a trail, as it were, for practical catechetical
efforts. I will use for this purpose a small representative portion of the *Catechism*. The christological catechesis is a likely example to choose. Because it would
take us too far afield to examine the whole of it point
by point, I would merely like to bring into relief a few
characteristic features of this catechesis, features that
also typify the theological line of the *Catechism* as a
whole.

The *Catechism* trusts the biblical word. It holds the
Christ of the Gospels to be the real Jesus. It is also
convinced that all the Gospels tell us about this same
Jesus and that all of them together help us, each in its
own way, to know the true Jesus of history, who is
no other than the Christ of faith.

This basic position has earned the *Catechism* vehe-
ment attacks. The *Catechism*, it is alleged, has slept
through an entire century of exegesis, is utterly ignorant of literary genres, form and redactional history,
and the like, and has not progressed beyond a "funda-
mentalistic" biblical exegesis.

It suffices to reread the chapter on the Bible and its

interpretation to see that this assertion is groundless.[24]
The *Catechism* quietly incorporates the truly solid results of modern exegesis. As evidence, I cite only the
chapter concerning the name of Jesus and the three
chief christological titles—Christ, Kyrios (Lord) and
"the Son"—a chapter that I count among the richest
and most profound texts of the *Catechism*.[25] However,
the many-layered, plastic portrayal of Jesus that modern research has uncovered in the Gospels in no way
forces us to go behind the texts and to construct another, allegedly purely historical Jesus from a combi-
nation of conjectured sources, while stigmatizing the
Gospel portrait of Jesus as a product of the community's faith. As to the further contention that different communities or representatives of the tradition be-

[24] CCC 101–41, esp. 109–19. It seems to me that there has never
been as substantial and comprehensible an introduction to the rudi-
ments of biblical science and interpretation in such a brief format.
Detailed statements on issues relating to the various levels of interpretation can be found in the document of the Pontifical Biblical Commission. Of the abundance of more recent exegetical literature on
this topic, I would like to mention here only T. Sternberg, ed., *Neue
Formen der Schriftauslegung?* (Freiburg, 1992). Given its catechetical
function, the *Catechism*'s reading of the Bible is essentially spiritual
interpretation. Spiritual here does not mean that the exegesis lacks re-
alism or disregards history but that it brings into view the spiritual
depth of the historical events. One could say that Christology and
pneumatology interpenetrate. "The Lord is the Spirit", says Paul (2
Cor 3:17). The *Catechism* repeatedly draws attention to this insepara-
bility of Christ and the Spirit (e.g., 485f.; 555), which is the presupposition of its method of spiritual reading.
[25] CCC 430–55.

lieved in different, incompatible Christs, it is hard to
see how such minimal historical reality, such a contra-
dictory mass of fabrications by the communities could
still produce in such a short time that common faith
in Christ that transformed the world.

In a recent series of publications, the great Jewish
scholar Jacob Neusner has vigorously opposed these
reconstructions and the concomitant devaluation of the
Gospels. This is not the place to review his arguments
in detail; let me simply cite the programmatic statement in which he sums up his own judgment, which
he bases on manifold evidence: "I write for believing
Christians and faithful Jews; for them, Jesus is known
through the Gospels."[26]

This is precisely the position of the *Catechism*; a
book that transmits the faith of the Church and does
not want to canonize private opinions can adopt no
other standpoint. Nor does this have anything at all
in common with fundamentalism, at the very least because a fundamentalist biblical exegesis excludes ecclesial mediation and accepts only the letter standing in
isolation.

When Neusner says in his study of Jesus that he
finds it impossible to argue with the Jesus imagined
by scholars because the historical figures they have
fabricated under that name are too numerous and too

[26] Neusner, *Rabbi Talks*, XV.

diverse,[27] he is alluding to a question whose urgency is felt more and more clearly in scientific exegesis itself. The school of canonical exegesis, whose importance is growing in America, insists emphatically that the primary task of all interpretation is to understand the given text as such. It must not evade this task by analyzing the text into its conjectured sources and in the end treating only of these. Of course, exegesis can and must also investigate the internal history of the texts in order to trace their development and thought patterns. We all know that there is much to learn from such work. But it must not lead us to neglect the principal task, which is to understand the text as it now stands, as a totality in itself with its own particular message.[28]

Whoever reads Scripture in faith as a Bible must make a further step. By its very nature, historical in-

[27] Ibid.: "Those fabricated historical figures are too many and diverse for an argument." A critical discussion of the attempts to reconstruct a historical Jesus can be found in V. Messori, *Ponzio Pilato*. Although polemical in parts, Messori's argument is always instructive not least because he takes into account what Jewish theologians are saying. A mediating position can be found in R. Schnackenburg, *Die Person Jesu Christi im Spiegel der vier Evangelien* (Freiburg, 1993), 348–54. Cf. also J. Gnilka, *Jesus von Nazareth*. Still fundamental for the right understanding of the underlying methodological question is H. Schlier, "Wer ist Jesus?" in: idem, *Der Geist und die Kirche* (Freiburg, 1980), 20–32.

[28] A basic orientation is offered by H. Gese, "Der auszulegende Text", in: idem, *Alttestamentliche Studien* (Tübingen, 1991), 266–82.

terpretation can never take us beyond hypotheses. After all, none of us was there when it happened; only
physical science can repeat events in the laboratory.
Faith makes us Jesus' contemporaries. It can and must
integrate all true historical discoveries, and it becomes
richer for doing so. But faith gives us knowledge of
something more than a hypothesis; it gives us the right
to trust the revealed Word as such.

It must be admitted that the dissolution of the biblical
witness about Jesus into a variety of fabricated per-
sonæ has led to a frightfully impoverished image of
Jesus and has rendered any living relationship with his
figure almost impossible. What remains of the image of
Jesus is often terribly meager. The American exegete
John P. Meier has given the first volume of his study
of Jesus the title *A Marginal Jew.*[29] What are we to
make of this? Can acquaintance with a marginal Jew
from a very distant past be "gospel", glad tidings?

The *Catechism*, reading the Gospels with faith-filled
courage as a many-layered and reliable whole, restores
to us an amazingly rich and vivid portrait of Jesus. We
rediscover as if for the first time how great the figure
of Jesus is, how it transcends all human measures and
precisely thus meets us in true humanity. Acquaintance

[29] J. P. Meier, *A Marginal Jew: Rethinking the Historical Jesus* (New
York: Doubleday, 1991); cf. on this, J. Neusner, "Who Needs the
Historical Jesus?" in: *The Right Guide* (1993), 32–34.

with this figure evokes joy: this is evangelization. We can talk again with this Jesus. He is not only a "program", the representative of a cause, whose remarkable poverty of content can only leave us perplexed. When I ask myself why our churches are emptying out, why our faith is trickling away, I would answer that one of the chief reasons is the evacuation of the figure of Jesus, coupled with the deistic conception of God. The more or less romantic ersatz Jesus currently being offered is not enough. He lacks reality; he is too far away. But the Jesus of the Gospels, whom we come to know again in the *Catechism*, is present because he is the Son and accessible to me because he is man. His human history is never merely a thing of the past; all of it is preserved in him and in the communion of his disciples as a thing of the present that still touches me today.

One more remark is worth making here. The *Catechism* has no trace of ecclesiocentrism. It has nothing to do with that astonishing reduction of Christian existence in which faith dwindles to ecclesial or parochial self-preoccupation, while the dream of a better Church to come is offered as a substitute for Christian hope. The Church is the place from which the *Catechism* thinks, the common subject that bears both authors and readers. But this subject does not look at herself. She exists precisely to give us those new eyes of faith without which we see nothing but distorted reflections of Jesus, not Jesus himself. The Church exists to let us see Christ and hear the Gospel.

A final remark. There is no passage of the *Catechism*'s christological catechesis that is mere intellectual theory. The whole of this catechesis aims at Christian living; it leads to prayer and the liturgy as the "presupposition of Christian life". The *Catechism*, because it is biblical, is also liturgically oriented, as the Fathers of the 1985 Synod requested. The titles of Christ issue in the language of prayer, as do the mysteries of the life of Jesus, from the expectation of Israel and the Gentiles to the Paschal Mystery.[30]

We find the ultimate foundation for our whole devotion to Jesus where the *Catechism* sums up the labors of the first seven ecumenical councils. On the basis of the Church's witness of faith, the fruit of a long, historical maturation, the *Catechism* ventures the bold statement: "Jesus knew and loved us each and all during his life, his agony, and his Passion and gave himself up for each one of us: 'The Son of God . . . loved me and gave himself [up] for me' [Gal 2:20]."[31]

---

[30] "*The Mysteries of Christ's Life*, CCC 512–70. This chapter of the *Catechism* has restored a long-lost main component of narrative Christology; cf. K. Rahner, "Mysterien des Lebens Jesu", *LThK* 7:721f.: on Thomas' treatment of the theme, see G. Lohaus, *Die Geheimnisse des Lebens Christi in der Summa theologiæ des heiligen Thomas von Aquin* (Freiburg, 1985).

[31] CCC 478.

Each one of us can and may apply to himself the dramatic personalization that Paul accomplishes in these words. Every man may say: The Son of God loved *me* and gave himself up for *me*.

Only with this statement does christological catechesis become gospel in the full sense of the word. We are not an indistinct mass before God. Christ does not and did not treat us as such. In all truth, Christ walked his path for me. This certainty is a grace given to accompany me in all the stages of my life, in my successes and failures, in my hopes and my suffering. He did all that he did for me and for every man who crosses my path in life: Jesus loved him, too, and gave himself up for him, just as he loved and loves me still. When we have learned to believe this again, when we are able to announce it to others as the message of truth, evangelization takes place. Then we know that the kingdom of God is near. And this knowledge gives us the strength to live and act out of this nearness.

Jesus of Nazareth, Israel and Christianity:

Their Relation and Their Mission according to the Catechism of the Catholic Church

The history of the relationship between Israel and Christianity is steeped in blood and tears. It is a history of mistrust and hostility, but also—thank God—a history interwoven with repeated initiatives of forgiveness, understanding and mutual acceptance.

Since Auschwitz, it has become fully clear that the task of reconciliation and acceptance is an imperative that we can no longer refuse. Auschwitz was the gruesome expression of a worldview that not only desired the destruction of Judaism but also despised, and attempted to blot out, the Jewish inheritance in Christianity. Nevertheless, this event leaves us wondering what caused the great historical enmity between those who ought to belong together because of their belief in the one God and their adherence to his will. Could we even go so far as to say that this enmity is a consequence of the Christian faith itself, of the "essence of Christianity", so that the attainment of real reconciliation would require the abandonment of that essence and the denial of the center of Christianity? This is a hypothesis that in recent decades Christian thinkers themselves have formulated in response to the horrors of history. The confession of Jesus of Nazareth as the Son of the living God, faith in the Cross as the redemption of humanity—do these things intrinsically imply a condemnation of the Jews as hardened and blinded, as guilty of the death of the divine Son? Supposing they did, would not the core of Christian faith itself oblige Christians to intolerance, indeed, to enmity, toward the Jews? Conversely, would not Jews, for the sake of their self-respect and in order to defend their historical dignity and deepest convictions, have to demand that Christians surrender the core of their faith—that is, would Jews not have to forswear tolerance as well? Is conflict programmed into the very heart of religion? Can it be overcome only through recantation?

These are the dramatic terms in which the problem is posed today. This shows that we are dealing with an issue that extends far beyond interreligious dialogue among academics and concerns the fundamental decisions of the present hour of history. There are increasingly frequent attempts to defuse the problem by portraying Jesus as a Jewish teacher who basically did not go beyond the scope of Jewish tradition. In this view, Jesus' execution can be accounted for by political tensions between the Jews and the Romans. And it is a fact that Jesus was executed by the Roman authorities, who inflicted on him the method customarily reserved for the punishment of political rebels. Jesus' exaltation to divine sonship, so it is said, occurred only later on, in a Hellenistic atmosphere—at about the same time that guilt for Jesus' death on the Cross was supposedly transferred from the Romans to the Jews out of political expediency. Such explanations can be a challenge to exegesis that compels it to heed the texts more closely, and in this way they may even be useful in a number of respects. However, these accounts do not say anything about the Jesus of the historical sources. Instead, they assemble a new and different Jesus. They banish the Church's historical faith in Christ to the realm of mythology, representing it as a product of Greek religiosity and political opportunism in the Roman Empire. Yet instead of coming to grips with the seriousness of the problem, this move avoids engaging it at all. The question thus remains: Can Christian faith, while remaining a serious and respectable proposition, not only tolerate Judaism but accept its historical mission—or can it not? Can there be true reconciliation without renouncing one's faith, or is such renunciation the necessary price of reconciliation?—Given that this question is something that concerns all of us very deeply, I am disinclined to present my own reflections on the matter. Instead, I will try to indicate how the *Catechism of the Catholic Church* explains it. The *Catechism* was promulgated by the Magisterium of the Catholic Church as an authentic expression of the Church's faith. At the same time, the *Catechism* has heeded both the warning of Auschwitz and the mandate of the Second Vatican Council: the cause of reconciliation, understood as a cause of the faith itself, is written into its very structure. Let us examine how the *Catechism* carries out this mandate in dealing with our question.

1. Jews and Gentiles as Reflected in the Story of the Wise Men from the East (Mt 2:1–12)

As an entry into the subject, I have selected the text in which the *Catechism* explains the story of the wise men from the East (Mt 2:1–12). For the *Catechism*, these men represent the origin of the Church of the Gentiles and permanently reflect her historical path. The *Catechism* makes the following remarks on the significance of the Magi:

> The magi's coming to Jerusalem in order to pay homage to the king of the Jews shows that they seek in Israel, in the messianic light of the star of David, the one who will be king of the nations [Mt 2:2]. Their coming means that pagans can discover Jesus and worship him as Son of God and Savior of the world only by turning toward the Jews and receiving from them the messianic promise as contained in the Old Testament. The Epiphany shows that "the full number of the nations" now takes its "place in the family of the patriarchs," and acquires *Israelitica dignitas* (are made "worthy of the heritage of Israel").[1]

[1] CCC 528.

This text shows how the *Catechism* understands the relationship mediated by Jesus between the Jews and the nations. In so doing, it likewise offers an initial treatment of the mission of Jesus himself. We could say in the light of this text that Jesus' mission is to bring Jews and Gentiles together into a single people that fulfills the universalistic promises of the Scriptures. These promises tirelessly announce that all the nations will worship the God of Israel. Indeed, in Trito-Isaiah we no longer merely read of the pilgrimage of the nations to Zion; we also find the announcement that messengers will be sent to the peoples "who have not yet heard of me or seen my glory. . . . And some of them also I will take for priests and for Levites, says the Lord" (Is 66:19, 21).

In order to explain how Jesus brings together Israel and the nations, our short text—still interpreting Matthew 2—gives a brief instruction on the relationship among the world's religions, the faith of Israel and the mission of Jesus. The world religions can play the role of the star that puts men on the path, that leads them to search for the kingdom of God. The star of the religions points toward Jerusalem; it is extinguished and relit in the Word of God, in the Holy Scripture of Israel. The Word of God preserved in Scripture appears as the true star, which we cannot dispense with or ignore if we wish to reach the goal. When the *Catechism* calls the star the "star of David", it further connects the story of the wise men to Balaam's prophecy concerning the star

that rises from Jacob (Nb 24:17). It sees this prophecy
linked in turn with Jacob's blessing of Judah, in which
he promises the staff and scepter to the one "to whom
the obedience of the peoples is due" (Gen 49:10). The
Catechism regards Jesus as this promised scion of Judah
who unites Israel and the peoples in the kingdom of
God.

What is the significance of the foregoing? What we
have said suggests that Jesus' mission is to unite the
histories of the nations in a common sharing in the history of Abraham, which is the history of Israel. Jesus'
mission is one of unification and reconciliation, as the
Letter to the Ephesians will later describe it (2:18–22).
Israel's history is destined to become the history of all
men, Abrahamic sonship is meant to be extended to
the "many". This event has two aspects. The nations
can enter into the community of the promises of Israel by entering into the community of the one God,
who now becomes—and must become—the way for
all men. This is because there is only one God and
because it follows from God's unicity that his will is
the truth for all. Conversely, this means that through
their covenantal integration into the will of God and
their acceptance of the Davidic kingship, all the nations
become, without abolition of the special mission of Israel, brothers and coparticipants in the promises to the
chosen people; indeed, they become the People of God
together with Israel.

A further observation is worth making here. As the *Catechism* interprets it, the story of the Magi represents Israel's sacred books as an oracle that offers the nations decisive, indispensable guidance in finding the right way. The narrative of the wise men thereby varies the motif that John's Gospel expresses in the words "salvation comes from the Jews" (4:22). That salvation comes from the Jews is a never-fading truth; no one can come to Jesus, hence, the nations cannot enter into the People of God, unless they accept in faith the revelation of God spoken in the Sacred Scriptures, which Christians call the Old Testament.

We can therefore recapitulate by saying that the Old and New Testaments, Jesus and the Holy Scriptures of Israel, appear inseparably joined together. The new dynamism of Jesus' mission, the bringing of Israel and the nations into unity, corresponds to the prophetic dynamism of the Old Testament itself. Reconciliation, which takes place in the common acknowledgment that God is king and that his will is our way, is the core of Jesus' mission. And in his mission, the person and the message are indivisible. This mission is already at work as Jesus lies, still wordless, in the manger. We have not understood him at all if we do not enter together with him into the dynamism of reconciliation.

2. *Jesus and the Law:*
Not Abolition, but "Fulfillment"

The grand vision of this text still leaves us, however, with a question about the historical realization of what the image of the star and the Magi anticipates. Does the historical picture of Jesus, along with his message and actions, match this vision, or does it not rather positively contradict it? Now, no question is more controverted than the question of the historical Jesus. The *Catechism*, as a book of faith, is guided by the conviction that the Jesus of the Gospels is also the only real Jesus of history. Presupposing this conviction, the *Catechism* first presents Jesus' message under the all-embracing heading "kingdom of God", which integrates the various aspects of his message, thus giving them their order and concrete content (541–60). The *Catechism* then displays the relation between Jesus and Israel in terms of three areas: Jesus and the law (577–82), Jesus and the Temple (583–86), Jesus and Israel's faith in the one God and Savior (587–91). Having treated this point, the *Catechism* finally moves to Jesus' final destiny—his death and Resurrection, which for Christians fulfills the Paschal Mystery of Israel and takes it to its ultimate theological depth.

The present discussion obliges us to focus particularly on the middle chapter concerning Jesus and Israel, a chapter that is also fundamental for interpreting the idea of the kingdom of God and for understanding the mystery of Easter. Now, the law, the Temple and the oneness of God are precisely the issues that cause the most explosive disagreements between Judaism and Christianity. Is there any chance at all that we can understand these subjects in a historically honest, religiously serious way, while at the same time acknowledging the primacy of reconciliation?

The generalizing portrayal of Pharisees, priests and Jews as negative figures is not peculiar to earlier interpretations of the history of Jesus. Liberal and modern accounts themselves have reestablished the cliché. The Pharisees and priests are depicted as the representatives of rigid legalism, of the unchanging law of the establishment, of the religious and political authorities, which interfere with freedom and thrive on the suppression of others. Correlative to these interpretations is the option to take Jesus' side and to champion his cause against priestly power in the Church and "law and order" in the state. The adversarial rhetoric of contemporary liberation movements fuses with images drawn from the history of Jesus. Indeed, this whole history is explained ultimately as a battle against religiously camouflaged domination of some men by others, as the beginning of that revolution in which Jesus was beaten yet by his very defeat made a beginning that must now lead to definitive victory. If we are to see Jesus in this light, if this state of affairs is to determine our understanding of

Jesus' death, then his message cannot be one of reconciliation.

It goes without saying that the *Catechism* does not share
this perspective. In these questions it takes Matthew's
presentation of Jesus as its chief guide and sees Jesus
as the Messiah, the greatest in the kingdom of heaven.
As such, Jesus knew that he was duty-bound "to fulfill the Law by keeping it in its all-embracing detail
—according to his own words, down to 'the least of
these commandments.' "[2] The *Catechism* thus connects
Jesus' special mission with his fidelity to the law; it
sees him as the servant of God who truly brings forth
justice (Is 42:3) and thereby becomes a "covenant for
the people" (Is 42:6).[3] At the same time, our text
is far from imposing a superficial harmony upon the
conflict-laden history of Jesus. However, instead of interpreting Jesus' mission—with equal superficiality—
as a so-called "prophetic" intervention against rigid legalism, the *Catechism* attempts to fathom its properly
theological depth. This becomes clear in the following
passage:

> This principle of integral observance of the Law not only
> in letter but in spirit was dear to the Pharisees. By giv-
> ing Israel this principle they had led many Jews of Jesus'
> time to an extreme religious zeal. This zeal, were it not

[2] CCC 578.
[3] Cf. CCC 580.

to collapse into "hypocritical" casuistry, could only pre-
pare the People for the unprecedented intervention of
God through the perfect fulfillment of the Law by the
only Righteous One in place of all sinners.[4]

This integral fulfillment of the law includes Jesus' taking upon himself the "curse of the law" (Gal 3:13) in-
curred "by those who do not 'abide by the things written in the book of the Law, and do them' (Gal 3:10)".[5]
With statements like these, the *Catechism* explains Jesus'
death on the Cross as flowing from a most intimate solidarity with the law and with Israel. In this context, it
refers to the Day of Atonement[6] and understands the
death of Christ itself as the great event of reconciliation, as the perfect accomplishment of the reality that
the signs of the Day of Atonement betokened.[7]

These statements bring us to the center of Christian-
Jewish dialogue, to the point where the paths to reconciliation and division diverge. However, before we
pursue the interpretation of Jesus' figure along the lines
that have begun to emerge here, we must first ask what
this view of Jesus' historical lineaments means existen-
tially for those who are conscious that through him
they have been engrafted into the "olive tree of Israel"
as sons of Abraham.

---

[4] CCC 579.
[5] CCC, 580.
[6] *Versöhnungstag*, lit., "day of reconciliation".—Trans.
[7] CCC 433; 578.

Those who present Jesus' conflict with the Judaism of his time in a superficial and polemical fashion tend to deduce from it a concept of liberation that can understand the Torah only as a servitude to exterior rites and observances. The *Catechism*'s vision, which is guided principally by Matthew's Gospel but ultimately by the totality of the Gospel tradition, leads logically to an entirely different conception, which I would like to quote at some length:

> The Law of the Gospel *fulfills the commandments* of the Law [=Torah]. The Lord's Sermon on the Mount, far from abolishing or devaluating the moral prescriptions of the Old Law, releases their hidden potential and has new demands arise from them: it reveals their entire divine and human truth. It does not add new external precepts, but proceeds to reform the heart, the root of human acts, where man chooses between the pure and the impure, where faith, hope, and charity are formed. . . . The Gospel thus brings the Law to its fullness through imitation of the perfection of the heavenly Father. . . . [8]

The *Catechism* reiterates the deep unity between Jesus' message and the message of Sinai in another passage referring to a New Testament enunciation that is not only common to the Synoptic tradition but also plays a central role in the Johannine and Pauline corpus: The whole law and the prophets hang on the double

[8] CCC 1968.

commandment to love God and neighbor.[9] The nations become Abraham's adopted children concretely when they enter into the one will of God, which inseparably unites the ethical commandments and the confession of the unicity of God. This becomes especially clear in Mark's version of the tradition, for Mark expressly ties the double commandment to the "Shᵉma Israel," the Yes to the one and only God. Man's way is already given: it is to measure himself against God's standard and God's own perfection. This likewise shows the ontological depth of these statements, for in giving his Yes to the dual commandment, man corresponds to the mission of his being, which the Creator intends as an image of God, and as such is realized when we love in communion with God's love.

Here we find ourselves beyond all historical and strictly theological discussions: we are squarely in the middle of the question of present-day Jewish and Christian responsibility before the modern world. This responsibility consists precisely in representing the truth of the one will of God before the world and thus in confronting man with his intrinsic truth, which is at the same time man's way. Jews and Christians must bear witness to the one God, to the Creator of heaven and earth. Moreover, they must do so in that totality which

[9] CCC 1970; cf., Mt 7:20; 22:34–40; Mk 12:38–43; Lk 10:25–28; Jn 13:34; Rom 13:8–10.

Psalm 19 formulates in exemplary fashion. The light of
the physical creation, the sun, and the light of the spirit,
the commandment of God, belong inseparably together.
The same God who speaks to the whole world in the
divine word and its radiance is the God who witnesses
to himself in the sun, moon and stars, in the beauty
and fullness of creation. "The sun is heaven's pride,
yet your law, Lord, much more beside."

3. Jesus' Interpretation of the Law: Conflict and Reconciliation

Now, however, the inevitable question arises: Does not
this view of the intrinsic connection between the law
and the gospel amount to an illegitimate concordism?
If this view is in fact true, how do we explain the
conflict that led to Jesus' crucifixion? Does not everything we have said contradict Paul's interpretation of
the figure of Christ? Are we not repudiating the entire
Pauline doctrine of faith in favor of a new moralism?
Have we not thereby done away with the "articulus
stantis et cadentis ecclesiæ",[10] hence, with the essential novelty of Christianity?

The *Catechism*'s text on morality, from which we
have drawn the foregoing remarks concerning the
Christian way, is at pains here to reflect the doctrine

[10] "The article by which the Church stands or falls."—TRANS.

that we took from the presentation of Christ in its dogmatic chapters. When we examine the matter closely, we see two essential aspects of this correspondence that give us the key to our questions.

a. The presentation of the intrinsic continuity and coherence of the law and the gospel set forth just now places the *Catechism* strictly within the Catholic tradition formulated especially by Augustine and Thomas Aquinas. This tradition has never regarded the relationship between the Torah and Jesus' preaching as a dialectic in which God appears in the law *sub contrario*,[11] as his own opponent, so to speak. This tradition has never favored dialectic but rather analogy, development within intrinsic correspondence, according to the beautiful sentence of Augustine: The New Testament lies hidden in the Old, the Old Testament lies open in the New. The *Catechism* cites a marvelous text from Thomas on the close interweaving that results from this relationship:

[11] This statement was interpreted by my listeners as an allusion to Luther's method of relating the two Testaments. In fact, I did have in mind certain aspects of Luther's thought, but I was of course also aware that a work as many-layered and as differentiated as that of the German Reformer cannot be expressed in any adequate way in a single sentence. Thus, there can and should be no question here of evaluating [*beurteilen*], let alone condemning [*verurteilen*], Luther's theology of the Testaments. The aim is simply to point out different models of treating the problem as a background against which the Augustinian-Thomist line adopted by the *Catechism* can be brought into sharper focus.

> There were . . . under the regimen of the Old Covenant,
> people who possessed the charity and grace of the Holy
> Spirit and longed above all for the spiritual and eternal
> promises by which they were associated with the New
> Law. Conversely, there exist carnal men under the New
> Covenant. . . .[12]

b. But the foregoing already implies a prophetic reading of the law in the light of the tension embedded in
the promise. The significance of this dynamic-prophetic
reading appears in the *Catechism* primarily in a double
movement wherein the law is brought to its fullness
through renewal of the heart,[13] while the outward effect of this fulfillment is the omission of the rituals and
juridical observances.[14] But at this point a new question
arises. How was this possible? How can this be squared
with the fulfillment of the law to the last iota? For
we cannot neatly divide universally valid moral princi-
ples from transitory ritual and legal ordinances without
destroying the Torah itself. The Torah is, after all, a
unitary structure pervaded by the recognition that it
came into being because God spoke to Israel. The no-
tion that, on one side, there is pure morality, which is
reasonable and universal, and, on the other side, time-
conditioned and ultimately dispensable rites is a complete misunderstanding of the characteristic structure

[12] CCC 1964; *S.Th.* I–II, 107, 1 ad 2.
[13] CCC 1968.
[14] CCC 1972.

of the five books of Moses. The Decalogue, the heart of the whole law, is clear enough proof that the separation between divine worship and morality, cult and ethics, is completely foreign to the law.

We thus come face to face with a paradox. Israel's faith was universal in scope. Directed toward the one God of all men, it also had the promise of becoming the faith of all nations. But the law wherein this faith was embodied was particular; its concrete reality was wholly relative to Israel and its history. The law could not be universalized in this form.

At the intersection of this paradox stands Jesus of Nazareth, who, himself a Jew, lived wholly within the law of Israel, while at the same time knowing that he was the mediator of this divine universality. This mediation could not come about through political calculation or philosophical interpretation. In either case, it would have been man who placed himself above God's word and reformed it according to his own criteria. Jesus did not act like a liberal who proposes a somewhat open-minded interpretation of the law that he then acts out. Jesus' conflict with the Jewish authorities of his time did not pit a liberal against an ossified traditionalist hierarchy. This common viewpoint is a radical misunderstanding of the conflict of the New Testament; it does justice neither to Jesus nor to Israel. The truth is that Jesus opened up the law in an entirely theo-logical way; he both knew and claimed that he was acting in the closest possible unity with God the Father; he both knew and claimed that he was acting as the Son endowed with God's own authority. Only God himself could reinterpret the law from the ground up as Jesus did; only God himself could show that the transformation and preservation that opened up the law had been the true intention of the law all along. Jesus' interpretation of the law makes sense only if it is an interpretation with divine authority, if it is God's own self-interpretation. The controversy between Jesus and the Jewish authorities of his time ultimately concerns, not this or that individual infraction of the law, but Jesus' claim to act *ex auctoritate divina*,[15] indeed, to be this *auctoritas* itself. "The Father and I are one" (Jn 10:30).

It is only when we come this far that we also see the tragic depth of the conflict. On the one hand, Jesus did not intend to—nor did he—open up the law in liberal fashion. His method was not to be less faithful to the law but to fulfill it integrally. This required the strictest possible obedience; it presupposed that unity with the Father that alone could unite the law and the promise, thus making Israel the blessing and the salvation of the nations. On the other hand, Israel "had to" see what Jesus did as something much graver than a trespass against this or that commandment. It "had

[15] "By divine authority."—TRANS.

to" regard it as the violation of the most fundamental obedience, of the authentic core of its revelation and faith, which is expressed in the words "hear, O Israel: The Lord our God is the one Lord." Here obedience clashes with obedience in a conflict that necessarily ends in the Cross. Reconciliation and division thus seem to be knotted together in a positively paradoxical way.

A consequence of what we have just said is that in this theology of the New Testament interpreted by the *Catechism* we cannot regard the Cross simply as an accident that could have been avoided. Nor does it allow us to see the Cross as the sin of Israel, which would now be eternally stained by it, but not of the Gentiles, for whom it would bring redemption. According to the New Testament, the Cross does not have two effects, one of damnation and the other of salvation, but only one effect—to save and reconcile.

In this connection there is an important text of the *Catechism* that interprets Christian hope as a continuation of Abraham's hope and in so doing links it with the sacrifice of Isaac. Accordingly, Christian hope "has its origin and model in the *hope of Abraham*". The text goes on to say that Abraham "was blessed abundantly by the promises of God fulfilled in Isaac and . . . was purified by the test of the sacrifice".[16] Through Abra-

---

[16] CCC 1819.

ham's willingness to sacrifice his son, he becomes the father of the many, a blessing for all the nations of the earth (cf. Gen 22). The *Catechism* thus indicates that from the very beginning the mystery of the Cross is inscribed in the hope of Abraham.

The New Testament sees the death of Christ in this perspective, as the consummation of the entire "law". It understands this law not simply as a collection of norms but as standing in the context of the whole biblical narrative, hence, as prophecy, as a way pointing ahead dynamically toward an ultimate—universal —sense that is yet to be unveiled. This means that all the cultic ordinances of the Old Testament are seen to be incorporated into this death and present in it and, in this way, brought to their deepest significance. All the sacrifices are, in fact, representative actions. In this great act of real representation they pass from symbol to reality, so that the symbols can fall away without the abandonment of a single iota. Jesus' universalization of the Torah, as the New Testament understands it, is not the extraction of a few universal moral prescriptions from the living totality of the revelation of God. This universalization retains the unity of cult and ethics. Ethics remains grounded and anchored in the worship of God. For in the Cross, the whole liturgy is concentrated, indeed, only in this concentration does it finally attain its full reality. According to Christian faith, Jesus opens and fulfills the totality of the law on the Cross. He presents it in this way to the Gentiles,

who are now also able to appropriate it in this totality
and thus become children of Abraham.

4. The Cross

This understanding of Jesus, his claim and his destiny is
the source of the *Catechism*'s historical and theological
judgment on the responsibility of Jews and Gentiles in
the crucifixion.

a. The first question is historical: How did Jesus' trial
and execution actually occur? The headings of the four
sections in which the *Catechism* treats of this question
already indicate the tenor of the answer: "Divisions
among the Jewish authorities concerning Jesus"; "Jews
are not collectively responsible for Jesus' death".

The *Catechism* recalls that, according to the testimony
of the Gospels, respected Jewish personages were ad-
herents of Jesus, that, as John tells us, shortly before
Jesus' death "many of the leading men came to believe"
(Jn 12:42). It also points out that, according to the account in Acts, on the day of Pentecost "a great many
of the priests were obedient to the faith" (6:7). The
Catechism also mentions James' statement that "many
thousands there are among the Jews of those who have
believed; and they are all zealous for the law" (Acts
21:20). The document further clarifies that the account
of Jesus' trial cannot be taken as grounds for affirming

any collective guilt on the part of the Jews. The Second Vatican Council is expressly cited: "Neither all Jews indiscriminately at that time, nor Jews today, can be charged with the crimes committed during his Passion. . . . [T]he Jews should not be spoken of as rejected or accursed as if this followed from Holy Scripture."[17]

b. It is clear from what we have just considered that such historical analyses—however important they may be—do not yet go to the real heart of the problem. For, according to the faith of the New Testament, Jesus' death is not a mere fact of empirical history but a theological event. The first heading in the *Catechism*'s theological analysis of the Cross thus reads as follows: "Jesus handed over according to the definite plan of God". The text itself begins with this sentence: "Jesus' violent death was not the result of chance in an unfortunate coincidence of circumstances, but is part of the mystery of God's plan. . . ."[18] Correspondingly, the *Catechism* concludes its inquiry into the question of responsibility for Jesus' death with a section entitled "All sinners were the authors of Christ's Passion."

In support of this affirmation, the *Catechism* could appeal to the Roman Catechism of 1566, where we read the following:

---

[17] CCC 597; *Nostra ætate*, 4.
[18] CCC 599.

When someone asks the reason why the Son of God took upon himself the bitterest suffering, he will find that, apart from the original sin of our first parents, it was principally the vices and sins that men have committed from the beginning of the world to this day and will commit from now until the end of the world. . . . We must regard as guilty all those who continue to relapse into their sins. Since our sins made the Lord Christ suffer the torment of the Cross, those who plunge themselves into disorders and crimes crucify the Son of God anew in their hearts (for he is in them) and hold him up to contempt (Heb 6:6).

The Roman Catechism of 1566, which the new *Catechism* cites, then adds that, according to the testimony of the Apostle Paul, the Jews did not understand "this; for if they had, they would not have crucified the Lord of glory" (1 Cor 2:8). It then continues: "We, however, profess to know him. And when we deny him by our deeds, we in some way seem to lay violent hands on him."[19]

For the believing Christian, who does not look upon the Cross as a sheer historical contingency but as a theological event in the strict sense, these are not superficial pieties to which we should have to oppose the realities of history. In fact, we have not penetrated into the true core of the events until we have taken these statements into account.

[19] *Roman Catechism*, I, 5, 11; CCC 598.

This core consists in the drama of man's sin and God's love; man's sin leads God's love for man to take the form of the Cross. On the one hand, sin is responsible for the Cross; on the other hand, the Cross is the overpowering of sin through God's more powerful love. Consequently, we must go beyond all questions of responsibility to the word of the Letter to the Hebrews (12:24) that expresses the ultimate truth of the matter: Jesus' blood speaks a different—better and stronger—language than the blood of Abel, than the blood of all those unjustly killed in the world. It does not cry out for punishment but is reconciliation.

Even as a child, I always found it incomprehensible—although I was of course unaware of all the recent discoveries that the *Catechism* brings together—that many people wanted to make Jesus' death a reason to condemn the Jews, for this word from Hebrews had penetrated my soul as a most profound consolation: Jesus' blood does not claim revenge but calls all to reconciliation [*Versöhnung*]; it has—as the Letter to the Hebrews shows—itself become the perpetual Day of God's Atonement [*Versöhnungstag*].

Concluding Remarks on the Common Task of Christians and Jews for the World

The foregoing considerations do not come even close to covering the whole compass of the subject proposed to us. They do no more than open up this vast expanse. In the light of the *Catechism* we have reflected on the relationship between Jesus and Israel, on the Church's faith in Christ, and on her relation to the faith of Israel. In treating this far-ranging subject, we have limited ourselves to a few basic elements that the *Catechism* proposes as guidelines for catechetical instruction in the Catholic Church. To be sure, we have thereby laid the foundations for the question of Israel and the Church, although to discuss them in detail would open a vast field, the elaboration of which would exceed the limits of this essay (not to mention the limits of catechetical teaching). Even less can we treat here the huge question of the common task of Jews and Christians in the contemporary world. Yet it seems to me that the core of this task appears through all that we have said and so suggests itself almost spontaneously: Jews and Christians should accept each other in a deep, reciprocal reconciliation. They should not do so by prescinding from their faith, let alone denying it, but should act out of the depth of their faith itself. In their mutual reconciliation, they should become a force of peace for the world. Through their testimony to the one God, who will not be worshipped except in the unity of love for God and love for neighbor, they should open to him the door into the world. They should open to him this door so that his will may be done, so that it may be on earth "as it is in heaven"—so that his "kingdom come".

Remarks on the Origin
of the Individual Chapters

The first of the four works printed here reproduces with slight modifications the text with which I presented the *Catechism* to the world press in Rome on December 9, 1992. The text has been printed in various newspapers and periodicals.

The second piece had a twofold purpose. It inaugurated a lecture series at the Roman University of Saint Thomas (the Angelicum) on January 15, 1993. I presented it again on January 18, 1993, in the Lateran Basilica on the occasion of the Synod of the diocese of Rome. This text was also reprinted in various newspapers and collections of lectures.

The third article was first drafted for the Commission for South America established at the Holy See. At the invitation of its president, Cardinal Gantin, and its vice-president, Archbishop Calderó, I wrote the piece for a plenary assembly of the Commission that was to gather in the fall of 1993 in order to take stock of the bishops' meeting that had convened the year before in Santo Domingo. The task facing the Commission was above all to search for ways to implement the decisions made in Santo Domingo. The theme of Santo Domingo had been *New Evangelization—Promotion of*

Man—Christian Culture. The assembled bishops had gone beyond the preceding conference at Puebla with their christological centering: faith in Christ was to be the starting point for all practical planning. Since the theme of evangelization linked the event of Santo Domingo to the *Catechism* published later in 1992, I was invited to explain evangelization from the perspective of the *Catechism* as a help to the Latin American bishops in connecting their pastoral program with the *Catechism* and in determining the place of the *Catechism* in it.

The resulting lecture was then given in somewhat differing versions at the University of Potenza and at the yearly meeting of Italian military chaplains in Ischia. I gave it in German in October 1993 at a meeting of priests on the occasion of the twenty-fifth anniversary of Archbishop Degenhardt's episcopal ordination. It was published as an offprint by the Archdiocese of Paderborn. I have reworked it for this book.

I developed the fourth piece for the great Jewish-Christian meeting that took place in February 1994 in Jerusalem under the competent and dynamic moderation of Rabbi Rosen. I had initially understood that the meeting was planned as a theological dialogue between Jews and Christians about their common and at the same time different, to some extent even antithetical, heritage. I had therefore proposed a lecture about the *Catechism*'s teaching on this common heritage. Only later did it become clear to me that the meeting was to focus not so much on religious dialogue between Christians and Jews as on the question of how to exercise religious leadership in a secularized world. The representatives of the individual communities were to speak on the basis of their experience; the participants then discussed all the presentations in workshops. But since the question of what we have in common could not be left entirely out of consideration, it seemed like a good idea to retain my original plan. In order to bring my remarks into line with the meeting as a whole, I tried to allude at the end, at least in a very brief concluding prospect, to the implications of the vision I had presented for the common responsibility of Jews and Christians in the secularized world. Finally, since my two guides in writing the text were the Bible and the *Catechism*, there seemed to be little point in filling it up after the fact with references to literature that could easily be tracked down elsewhere.